S.S. 550 A.]

Ia/12828

NOTES AND ILLUSTRATIONS
ON THE INTERPRETATION
OF AEROPLANE PHOTOGRAPHS

Series A

ISSUED BY THE GENERAL STAFF.

FireStep
Editions

www.firesteppublishing.com

FireStep Publishing
Gemini House
136-140 Old Shoreham Road
Brighton
BN3 7BD

www.firesteppublishing.com

First published by the General Staff, War Office 1917.
First published in this format by FireStep Editions,
an imprint of FireStep Publishing, in association with
the National Army Museum, 2013.

NATIONAL
ARMY
MUSEUM
www.nam.ac.uk

ISBN 978-1-908487-85-8 PB
ISBN 978-1-908487-87-2 HB

Cover design FireStep Publishing
Typeset by FireStep Publishing
Printed and bound in Great Britain

Please note: *In producing in facsimile from original historical documents,
any imperfections may be reproduced and the quality may be lower than modern
typesetting or cartographic standards.*

ABOUT THIS SERIES

The First World War was a conflict fought on many fronts and on a truly industrial scale. At home men and women toiled to produce everything that was necessary to equip, sustain and arm the men in the war zones. The Edwardian era had seen significant advances in both science and technology. These scientific and technological advances would be utilised at every level - at the front line, in the Lines of Communication and on the Home Front.

In November 1918 the strength of the British and Colonial Forces was estimated to be 5,336,943 troops. Each of these had to be equipped, fed, to know how to operate equipment, to know how to fight and much more to perform all the tasks needed to fulfil the requirements an Army needs to function. This did not "just happen". Men had to train to learn how to use their equipment and they had to practice the roles they were expected to perform. Only when they were proficient in both could they then be sent to their various units as trained soldiers.

To help explain how all these tasks, as diverse as the care of horse equipment to dealing with unexploded shells, bombs and grenades were carefully studied and documented in a series of publications, which were circulated to explain, often in great detail how the various technical, tactical, organisational and many other functions could and should be performed.

A key advantage in warfare is to understand what your enemy is doing, what they intend to do and how they intend to do it. The role of those involved in military intelligence is to evaluate, analyse and interpret information about the enemy. To help with information gathering, interpretation and use of this information, publications are produced to explain how subjects on how the enemy is organised, enemy tactics and doctrine and how enemy equipment and weapons work and are operated.

These documents provide a fascinating insight into the daily lives of soldiers, as well as details of how the conflict was fought. They also help to dispel the myth that the First World War was fought on a basis of tactical and organisational mismanagement. On the contrary, every functional detail was carefully thought through, explained and documented.

They tell the true story of how the British Army fought and provide a detailed, factual insight for anyone with an interest in the "War to end all Wars".

Mark Khan
Series Editor
FireStep Publishing

INTRODUCTION

It is perhaps the feats of the flying aces that are widely remembered with regards aeroplanes and the First World War. But as Arthur Gould Lee reminds us in his book *No Parachute*, the Royal Flying Corps was largely:

> 'made up of ordinary young men doing their job without thought of glory, who bore the main burden of the air war, who carried out the unglamorised [sic] routine duties – the artillery observation, the reconnaissance, the photography, the bombing, and the endless protective fighter patrols' (Gould Lee 1969: 17).

Aerial photography was a fledgling development and this 1917 General Staff publication draws us into a world where aviators risked their lives to take photographs as they extended the battlefield zone to the air to become the eyes of the Army. Low oblique photographs, in particular, were very difficult to take because the aeroplane had to be flown closer to the ground exposing the aviator to enemy fire requiring him to resist the natural urge to flee from danger as his sense of duty took hold – he had to return with the photographs he was tasked to take, but they had to be taken with a steady hand for clear and, therefore, useful results.

As an archaeologist, such photographs are particularly interesting to me because O.G.S. Crawford, an observer in the Royal Flying Corps, was so impressed with the possibilities of air photography as an aid to finding and identifying archaeological sites, that he was instrumental in introducing aerial photography to landscape archaeology.

It is wonderful to see this book reprinted for it is quite unique. It offers a visual record of the war on the ground from the air, instructing, through the mode of annotated aerial photographic examples and pen and ink illustrations, how Royal Flying Corps staff should interpret aerial photographs to identify military features such as: gun emplacements; railway and trench tramways; buried cables and airlines; dug-outs and mine shafts; trench construction; and warning indications of a raid or attack. It also reveals that there was more to photographic interpretation than meets the eye! For example, there is an intriguing photograph of a training model that was constructed from an old cigarette tin, a wooden match box and a small amount of cement. The model is of a trench mortar emplacement before the salvage parties had removed the trench mortar ammunition. The model was dusted with table salt to give the appearance of earth as shown on a photograph. Copies and a description of the photograph were circulated to be compared with emplacements of a similar appearance along the front.

This is a real gem of a book. It informs and intrigues, even more so now that the two companion volumes (*notes on the interpretation* and *illustrations to accompany notes on*) have been combined into one concise publication.

Melanie R. Winterton
PhD Candidate, Department of Archaeology and Anthropology,
University of Bristol, October 2013

S.S. 550.]
[IA/12828.

NOTES ON THE INTERPRETATION OF AEROPLANE PHOTOGRAPHS.

Revised March, 1917.

ISSUED BY THE GENERAL STAFF.

CONTENTS.

(NOTE.—The plate numbers refer to " Illustrations to accompany Notes on the Interpretation of Aeroplane Photographs," Series A.)

The following notes, which have been prepared by the General Staff, are issued in order to facilitate the accurate location of important military features by means of aeroplane photographs; they amplify and supersede the notes contained in S.S. 445 (issued in November, 1916). The photographs have been selected by the Armies concerned, and represent the different natures of ground on the whole front between the Sea and the Oise.

These notes should be studied in conjunction with S.S. 537, "Summary of recent information regarding the German Army and its methods," Chapters I., II. and VI.

GENERAL STAFF (INTELLIGENCE),
GENERAL HEADQUARTERS,
March, 1917.

NOTES ON THE INTERPRETATION
OF AEROPLANE PHOTOGRAPHS.

I.—GENERAL.

I. The examination of photographs.—Before commencing the examination of photographs, every opportunity should be taken of studying on the ground objects similar to those which may require to be identified on a photograph. Thus, captured hostile trenches and positions should be visited until the different types of German works become thoroughly familiar.

The configuration and nature of the ground should be studied in order that a correct impression may be gained of the siting of the features on a photograph.

Every opportunity should also be taken of studying the ground from the *air*.

During the actual examination of a photograph, the following points should be remembered ; they are placed in order of importance :—

(a) Study the best available map with great care, so that the configuration of the ground and the salient details are thoroughly familiar. During the whole examination of the photograph, keep the map with you for constant comparison with the photograph.

(b) Ascertain the direction of light.

(c) Concentrate your whole mind on the particular objects which you are seeking. Do not let your attention wander to subsidiary objectives. Follow every traverse and detail with a pointer in regular and logical order, but be careful not to mark the photograph.

(d) Examine the photograph as an item of independent evidence and then compare this evidence with reports of visual observation, locations given in Intelligence Summaries, and evidence of reliable prisoners. Eliminate those portions of this evidence which are obviously wrong ; consider the likely places for the objects referred to in the remainder, and verify them. Avoid "special pleadings" and do not allow yourself to read in a photograph what you *want* to see.

(e) Compare the photograph with earlier photographs of the same locality ; it is from such comparisons that valuable results are obtained. This applies in particular to the appearance of objects on a photograph as affected by the changes of season.

(f) Be particularly careful to avoid obliterating detail when annotating or marking photographs.

2. Shadow.—Shadow plays a most important part in the interpretation of photographs. It is essential to ascertain the direction of light in order to decide whether the point under osbervation is convex or concave, and in order to get an idea of the depth or height of cuttings and embankments by comparison with the length of shadow cast by other objects.

3. Alterations in detail.—New photographs are useful in discovering alteration in old detail, as for instance the comparison between an old cadastral plan and a recent photograph, showing how a road has been altered in the course of time.

4. Necessity for verifying doubtful points.—A great deal of the patience and care taken in the study of aeroplane photographs is wasted unless verification of doubtful points is obtained from the inspection of captured trenches. It is not enough for a few people to view these points. A more practical and quite a simple way is to make a model of them before the machine guns or trench mortars have been removed and the emplacements dismantled.

II.—MACHINE GUNS.

1. Machine gun emplacements.—Emplacements for machine guns are either open or covered. Both types are difficult to locate with certainty. In examining photographs, special attention should be paid to any traverse, the size, shape or angle of which departs from the normal. Oblique photographs are a valuable aid in discovering machine gun emplacements.

2. The open emplacement takes the form of a square tray or concrete platform let into the parapet. It varies in appearance according to the altitude of the sun, and may show up either as a white mark with a dark edge or as a comparatively dark square. The latter is hard to distinguish from the many dark nicks in the parapet, which may be sentry posts or firing recesses.

3. The covered emplacement, which is concreted or otherwise strengthened, should be the object of particular attention, as it requires special treatment at the hands of our artillery and trench mortars, when once located. Though the use of covered emplacements is tending to diminish, a certain number may be expected in each sector. Their sites are selected with a view to :—

(a) A good field of fire (preferably enfilade).

(b) Concealment from direct observation from the immediate front.

(c) Rapid removal of the machine gun.

5

For the above reasons, they may be looked for :—

      (i.) Where an angle occurs in the trench system within convenient reach of a communication trench, with dug-outs for the gun crew close at hand.

      (ii.) Close to the base of a well-protected sap, from the head of which a sentry can give warning and prevent the gun from being rushed.

      (iii.) Occasionally behind the parados.

A covered emplacement may be discovered by a "V" shaped mark in the forward edge of the parapet, where the latter has been cut away to allow the gun to traverse. At the back of this "V," or close beside it in the trench if the emplacement is entered from the side, may be found a dark nick similar to a dug-out entrance. Sometimes a very short trench is cut out to it.

At times the position of a covered emplacement is revealed by a square mark on the forward slope of the parapet ; this occurs when the sun is shining at a slight angle behind the opening, but not at a sufficient angle to show up the "V."

III.—TRENCH MORTARS.

1. Types.—The Germans use various types of trench mortar, of which the regulation rifled patterns are the light, medium and heavy.

2. Siting.—The following are likely sites for trench mortar emplacements :—

      (a) In the shallow disused trenches which often exist behind the German fire trenches, a portion of which is deepened to take the mortar.

      (b) Immediately in front of the parapet of a fire trench.

      (c) By the side of a communication trench.

      (d) Along or near the terminus of a trench tramway (especially in the case of heavy trench mortars).

Many trench mortar emplacements can be found by following a line drawn parallel to our own front line at a distance of about 500 yards. Others must be searched for anywhere up to about 700 yards from our front line.

3. Light trench mortar emplacements.—Light trench mortars are often fired from open emplacements to allow a rapid change of position, and it is difficult to distinguish their emplacements from latrines or store pits. One difference, which is by no means universal, is that trenches leading to trench mortar emplacements are more often zig-zagged or traversed than in the case of trenches leading to latrines. It is only by close co-operation with ground observers that these emplacements can be definitely located.

4. Medium and heavy trench mortar emplacements are casemated and much more conspicuous. They can generally be recognized by an almost square, darkish mark in the centre of a mound or ring of earth. This square mark is the top of the funnel up which the mortar fires, and differs in appearance according to the angle of light ; it may be black, diagonally black and grey, or grey with a short, oblong, dark slit.

IV.—BATTERIES.

1. The location of batteries as affected by topographical conditions.—Types of battery emplacements, and the degree of difficulty in locating them accurately, differ according to the topographical features on the various sectors of the front. The area opposite the British may be divided as follows :—

      (a) The thickly populated mining area.

      (b) Close country with scattered houses, frequent woods, hedges and orchards.

      (c) Closely wooded country.

      (d) Country intersected by ravines and sunken roads.

      (e) Open country.

(a) *In the mining area,* the ground is usually broken, and numerous dumps and quarries afford cover. The house problem is a difficult one. Sections of a battery or single guns may be detached and placed irregularly. In "Cités," the houses are of stereotyped pattern, and may all have been knocked about. *Débris* litters the ground and helps to conceal tracks or traces of frequent use. Guns are placed in casemates in a house, a portion of which is pulled down over them to give extra cover; this has the effect of giving the house an appearance similar to that of any other ruined building in the vicinity.

(b) *In close and flat country,* in addition to houses, there are many hedges and orchards which afford good battery positions. Fields are bounded by ditches, which are not always shown on the map, thus rendering location difficult.

(c) *In wooded country,* especially if the woods are of any extent, batteries are difficult to locate with accuracy owing to the fact that, just when conditions are most favourable for air photography (i.e., in spring and summer), the leaves and natural cover are thickest. Camouflage with fresh branches and undergrowth is a simple matter, and tracks which can be seen entering a wood are soon lost inside it.

(d) *In country intersected by ravines and sunken roads,* batteries can be dug into the sides of a ravine or road and well hidden. The roads are all more or less used, because they afford natural cover, and signs of extra use at any point are not too apparent.

(e) *In open country*, where there are few villages and woods, batteries are almost invariably dug in and provided with heavy cover. For this reason they are more obvious, except where special care is taken to incorporate them into existing trenches.

2. Types of emplacement.—Apart from batteries in houses, emplacements are best considered in two categories—normal and abnormal.

Normal emplacements are almost invariably casemated and provided with heavy cover. They may be classified roughly as :—

(a) Trench emplacements, *i.e.*, with the gun pits built into existing trenches or into specially constructed trenches.

(b) Emplacements entirely dug in in the open and concealed by various artificial devices.

(c) Emplacements dug into road banks, ravines or hedges.

(d) Emplacements in woods.

Abnormal emplacements are few in number and are better illustrated than described.

3. Construction.—The principal object is to provide cover for men as well as guns, and it may be taken for granted that, unless the battery is in or on the edge of a village, where the personnel can be billeted in an adjacent house or cellar, each battery will have dug-outs and ammunition stores close to or adjoining the pits. These dug-outs may be at either end of the position, in between the pits or close at hand. In nearly every case they will be as heavily protected as the pits themselves.

An increasingly common feature with batteries in exposed positions is a covered trench leading from an adjacent road or trench, enabling personnel and ammunition to enter the battery without leaving tracks above ground.

It is important to note the grouping of pits, which are not always equally spaced.

When batteries are forced to retire, the Germans have almost invariably constructed emplacements of the normal type in the new position. It has been exceptional to find guns firing in the open.

4. Concealment.—It is evident that increasing care is taken to conceal emplacements and to defeat the camera. As, however, the Germans usually start to construct camouflage after a battery emplacement has been completed, their attempts are rendered abortive, owing to the fact that the emplacement will probably have been photographed several times during the various stages of construction.

Blast marks made by the guns help to defeat camouflage. Under ordinary conditions, they show up as white scores where the surface has been blown away by the discharge, or, in snow photographs, as black smudges. In dry weather, blast marks may be visible for some time after the position has been vacated, and are therefore not a proof that an emplacement is occupied. In themselves they only prove that a position *has been* active, not that it *is* active—a distinction which is liable to be forgotten.

Photographs have, however, proved that an emplacement is active :—

(a) By an immediate snow photograph.

(b) By a photograph of the guns actually firing.

V.—RAILWAYS AND TRENCH TRAMWAYS.

Much information of tactical and strategical importance can be gained from a close study of railways and trench tramways.

1. Employment.—Besides the normal gauge lines, which were mostly built before the war, the Germans have made an extensive use of the light railway system in the occupied portions of France and Belgium, and have extended this system near the front by new construction on a large scale. Personnel, stores and material are brought up by branch lines, which run to nearly all important points and villages in the front line system, and battery groups and single heavy batteries are almost entirely supplied by this method. Supply dumps will almost necessarily occur at the breaks of gauge, as well as at various points along the tracks.

2. New construction.—The light railway systems may be divided into three groups :—

(i.) 1·00 m. and 0·80 m. gauge, of which the former is the more common.

(ii.) 0·60 m. gauge.

(iii.) 0·40 m. gauge.

In the first of these groups, new work has consisted in extending the existing lines in operation before the war. The second and third groups have come into existence since the commencement of trench warfare, and are found only in the forward areas.

As far as possible, 0·60 m. gauge has been used in all new work, as this standard lends itself for several reasons to the requirements of field warfare.

Metre gauge has, as a general rule, been used in new construction only where lines of that gauge already existed, and where the use of a different standard would cause needless transhipment. The use of 0·40 m. gauge is restricted to the more forward trench tramways where mechanical traction is rarely used

The German forward railway systems are constantly being altered, especially during active operations. Light lines spring into being to serve a definite purpose, such as the construction of a new line of defence or the regrouping of artillery, and are taken up as soon as they are no longer required. The mark of the track remains for some time after the rails and sleepers have been removed, and photographs of such areas should be carefully examined for signs of deterioration or disuse.

3. Characteristic appearance on a photograph.—*Light railways* (1·00, 0·80 and 0·60 m. gauge) can be distinguished on a photograph by:—

    (*a*) The straightness with which they run.

    (*b*) The absence of any series of sharp curves.

    (*c*) Embankments and cuttings at points in their construction.

    (*d*) Bridges by which they cross streams or trenches.

They will also follow contours and defiladed ground.

Trench tramways (0·40 m. gauge) may be recognized by :—

    (*a*) The narrowness of the track, which shows as a fine line on the photograph, probably owing to the natural inclination of men to walk between the rails.

    (*b*) Their sharper curves where they continue into the trench system.

    (*c*) The absence of traverses in the trench in which they are laid.

Railways have a tendency to appear darker on a photograph than used roads or tracks.

VI.—TRACKS.

Tracks form a valuable guide to the enemy's movements, but are sometimes neglected because they are obvious.

The clues which they afford deserve enumeration :—

    (1) They disclose routes from railhead to billets and from billets to trenches. Even after the trenches are reached, the main communication trenches may be distinguished by tracks running alongside, made by carrying parties at night, or by working parties employed in the upkeep of important trenches.

    (2) They throw light on the limits of sectors, the study of which is important.

    (3) They disclose dumps ; battery positions ; headquarters ; wire which is otherwise invisible, and gaps through it ; patrol paths ; observation posts ; in villages, those houses which are important centres ; advanced listening posts ; fortified shell holes ; in suitable weather when tracks show up immediately, the activity of working parties.

As in the case of railways, the traces of tracks remain for a long time, and photographs should be examined for signs of disuse, such as new and continuous wire, or broad and unbridged trenches passing across them.

The value of a combined study of tracks and railways in giving assistance to machine guns and artillery for indirect fire, especially at night, is obvious. When made special targets during more important operations, the resulting confusion and disorganization of the enemy's system has proved very serious to him.

VII.—BURIED CABLES AND AIR LINES.

1. The study of cable trenches and air lines.—It is important that buried cables and air lines should be marked down when fresh, as they tend to disappear quickly, and in course of time become more and more invisible. They should be studied in conjunction with railways and tracks, as they all come under the heading of communications.

2. Cable trenches are a valuable aid in discovering the positions of headquarters, telephone dug-outs, camouflaged batteries, observation posts and important centres. Where the buried cables end, the air line system can be picked up.

Cable trenches can be distinguished, when open, by their more or less straight course and narrow construction, and when filled in by their irregular definition and somewhat " woolly " appearance. Where they cross over other trenches, a gap appears, as the lines are passed under the trench flooring.

3. Air lines appear as a series of regular white dots, these being the displaced earth where the poles have been erected. These dots are connected by a thin white track, which is made by the men walking from pole to pole putting up the wire or patrolling the line.

Air lines will sometimes come to life again on a photograph if the ground has been cultivated or ploughed, and they then show up as a succession of small dark islands, where the soil round the posts has not been disturbed. In clear photographs the shadows thrown by the poles can be seen.

VIII.—DUG-OUTS AND MINE SHAFTS.

1. Dug-outs can be detected in several ways, especially in a photograph taken while they are under construction. It is then possible to see the entrances to the shafts. These appear as black nicks, usually in the corners on either side of a traverse, where the maximum amount of protection from shell fire is afforded.

When dug-outs are made, a large amount of earth is thrown out which varies with their depth. This earth is apparent on older photographs.

Increasing care, however, is now being taken to conceal defences, and the earth thrown out is frequently well scattered and quickly becomes difficult to trace.

If the photograph is sufficiently clear and the light falls favourably, it will still be possible to see the black nicks which represent the entrances. These are still clearer if the point where the fire step has been cut through can be seen.

In snow photographs, dug-outs under construction are very obvious.

2. **Mine Shafts** show a similar black nick in the traverse, but their location is more difficult. The entrances are sometimes protected by splinter-proof cover built across the trench.

An indication of their presence is the large amount of spoil brought up from the galleries and spread about in the vicinity.

IX.—TRENCH CONSTRUCTION AND GENERAL DEFENSIVE SYSTEM.

Trench construction may be considered under the following headings :—

(1) Stationary or trench warfare, with steady and methodical additions and improvements to defences.

(2) Special trench construction indicating that an attack is anticipated.

(3) Special trench construction indicating that an attack is intended.

(4) Construction of defences during a battle.

In case (1), photographs can be studied at length and more or less at leisure.

In cases (2) and (3), there will be at least a few days for study.

In case (4), only a rapid investigation of photographs is possible, requiring a quick decision regarding, and immediate dissemination of points of interest.

1. **Stationary or trench warfare.**—(a) *General organization of a German Position.* At least two, but more often three, successive positions or systems of defence are prepared, each position consisting of two or more continuous lines. These lines include strong points such as villages, farms or woods which may happen to be situated in the forward area. In fact, the normal procedure, when taking up a new position, is to fix on a general line of natural strong points, and to prepare these for defence first, and then to join them up by fire trenches. The first indication that a new line is being constructed is usually the appearance of trenches covering villages and woods.

Support and reserve lines usually include a number of closed works, heavily wired, full of dug-outs, and with a liberal supply of communication trenches to facilitate the speedy passage of the garrison to any threatened point.

(b) *The determination of sector boundaries.* The division of a defensive system into sectors and sub-sectors affords a study of considerable importance. At intervals in the front-line trench, short sections may be found where the amount of earth thrown up is noticeably small. These may indicate the permanent limits of a company sector. There is a natural tendency for a company to commence work about the centre of its sector, leaving the flanks until the last, in case any subsequent alteration in the sector limits should result in another company enjoying the benefit of its labours.

Each sector is fed by several communication trenches, decreasing in number in proportion as the distance from the first line increases. Between the first trench and the second and third trenches of the front-line position, there are many communication trenches. Between the front-line position and the second-line position there may be more, but scarcely ever less than two main feeders—an IN track and an OUT track. There are generally two from the second-line position to the third-line position or to rest billets.

From a study of the map and photographs, determine the two main communication trenches. Compare the latter with the tracks that converge on or run beside them, and note where these tracks branch off to the front-line trench. An examination of the points where the branch tracks end should give the approximate limit of the sector. Draw a pencil line through this point, and proceed to construct the next sector. Three of these sectors will give the regimental boundaries of a Divison.

It will be found that each sector is like a human hand and arm, with the main arteries running down the arm and feeding the spread fingers through the smaller veins which lead to the finger tips and return.

Topographical features, such as canals, rivers, main roads or railway lines, occasionally form natural divisions between sectors and enable one boundary to be determined.

2. **Indications that an attack is anticipated.**—The following are indications that an attack is anticipated :—

(a) New lines of barbed wire, behind which occasional traverses and dug-outs appear, marking the trace of an intended new line.

(b) General strengthening and deepening of trenches.

(c) Addition to existing wire.

(d) Rapid construction of intermediate and switch lines.

(e) An increase in battery positions.

3. Indications that an attack is intended.—The following are indications that an attack is intended :—

(a) A sudden increase of artillery activity or in the number of battery positions.

(b) An increase in the number of communication trenches.

(c) A series of saps pushed forward and hastily linked up.

(d) Possibly, in the case of small attacks, new assembly trenches in or behind the front line trenches, or numerous small **T** shaped trenches or recesses for holding extra groups of men belonging to the second wave of the assault.

(e) A rapid increase in the number of light railways.

4. During a battle.—The conditions during a battle render the interpretation of aeroplane photographs far more difficult, for the following reasons :—

(a) Artillery preparation and continuous bombardment cut up the ground and obliterate trenches and landmarks.

(b) Battery positions are destroyed or captured, and new ones appear everywhere.

(c) New lines of defence may be scattered, and may consist merely of a line of fortified shell holes; these may be either detached, or improved and linked up to form part of a new defensive organization in conjunction with any available natural cover.

The following are some of the more important points which should be looked for :—

(i.) Tracks into shell holes which may contain detached parties or machine guns.

(ii.) Old battery positions, many of which are wired round and, when occupied by infantry, will form local strong points.

(iii.) Blocks and barricades across communication trenches.

(iv.) New tracks across country.

(v.) New active battery positions.

X.—OBLIQUE PHOTOGRAPHS.

Oblique photographs give a view such as an observer from a high hill is accustomed to see. Hence, though necessarily somewhat distorted, they convey more information to the unskilled student of air photographs than do vertical photographs.

They disclose details such as machine gun emplacements otherwise hidden, identify individual trees of which only the tops can otherwise be seen, and indicate the contours of the country.

They also give valuable assistance in working out the heights of embankments and the depths of sunken roads.

XI.—STEREOSCOPIC EFFECT WITH AIR PHOTOGRAPHS.

1. Method of use.—When any locality is photographed, two or more exposures are often made in order to ensure that one plate at least covers the area. Very often two or more of them do so, and may give a stereoscopic effect if looked at through a stereoscopic viewer.

To obtain this effect, take the two photographs of the object (two copies of the same photograph will not do—a fact which is not always recognized), and place one photograph on the top of the other, so that the features on one coincide with the same features on the other.

Draw the top photograph aside, keeping the features under examination parallel the whole time, until at about 2 inches apart the images will again fit, and houses and trees will stand up as in nature.

The photographs must be placed in the order in which they were taken, i.e., the left hand picture on the left side, as otherwise the features will appear reversed and houses will sink into holes, and cuttings will become embankments.

At first the number of images may be confusing, but a few minutes' practice will be enough to accustom the eyes to pick up the two required.

2. Value.—Stereoscopic photographs reveal, for example, depressions and slopes which are not distinguishable on a vertical single photograph.

By showing up objects in relief, they enable the artillery to estimate the amount of cover over emplacements and the nature of their protection, thus materially assisting them to determine what nature and calibre of gun is required to deal with them effectively.

S.S. 550 A.]

Ia/12828

ILLUSTRATIONS TO ACCOMPANY

NOTES ON THE INTERPRETATION
OF AEROPLANE PHOTOGRAPHS.

Series A.

ISSUED BY THE GENERAL STAFF.

A.P. & S.S.

ILLUSTRATIONS TO ACCOMPANY NOTES ON THE INTERPRETATION OF AEROPLANE PHOTOGRAPHS.

SERIES A.

LIST OF PLATES.

(NOTE.—*The title of each plate refers only to the particular feature which it is desired to illustrate. Many similar features occur on other plates, but have not necessarily been annotated on the diagrams.*)

PLATE 1.

CONVENTIONAL SIGNS FOR USE ON AEROPLANE PHOTOS.

Meaning.	Sign.	Instructions.
Machine Gun	M.G.	
Trench Mortar	⊙	
Dugout	▭	
Observation Post	O.P.	
Wire Entanglements	✕ ✕	Crosses widely spaced shown in front of line of wire
Gap or path in wire	⌒	A thin line drawn parallel to actual track.
Dump	△	
Battery	⌣	Drawn in front of and parallel to position.
Battery A.A.	∅	
Listening Post	L.P.	
Buried Cable	— . —	
Overhead Cable	— • —	Drawn at intervals alongside the line, just clear of it.
Tramway	—+—	
Probable Tank Traps	◇	
New Work	NEW	

NOTE - *The sign to be written clear of the object on the photo. with a detached arrow pointing to it. (when necessary.)*

PLATE 2.

DIAGRAM ILLUSTRATING THE RECONSTRUCTION, FROM THEIR SHADOWS, OF FIVE CIRCULAR OBJECTS SEEN VERTICALLY FROM ABOVE.

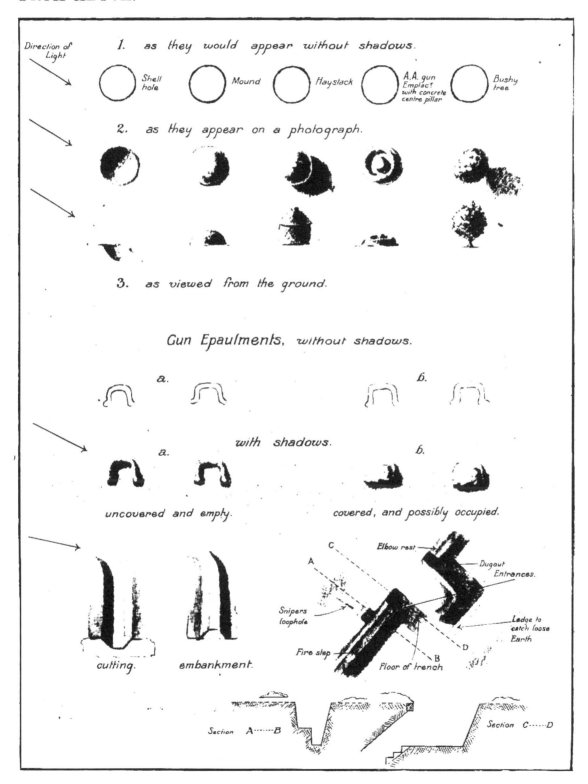

PLATE 3.

MACHINE GUN EMPLACEMENT.

1. Front and side view, without shadows.

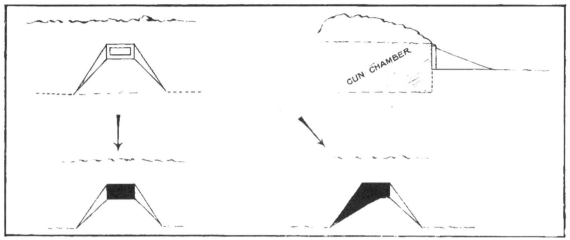

2. Front view, with light above.   3. Front view, with light at side.

DIAGRAM SHOWING PLAN OF CONSTRUCTION, HEAD COVER
AND METHOD OF STORING AMMUNITION, FROM CAPTURED EMPLACEMENTS NEAR FRICOURT.

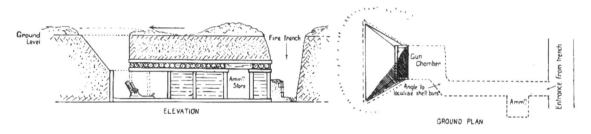

TRENCH MORTAR EMPLACEMENTS, SHOWING DIFFERENCE IN
APPEARANCE ACCORDING TO DIRECTION OF LIGHT.

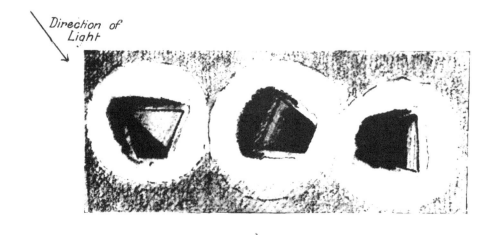

Plate 4.

GOOD PHOTOGRAPHS FOR BEGINNERS.

AREA :—River Ancre to River Somme.

La Bassée Canal to River Scarpe.

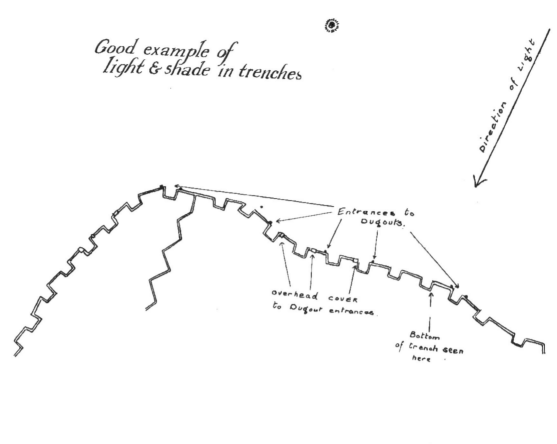

Good example of
light & shade in trenches

Direction of Light

Entrances to Dugouts.

overhead cover
to Dugout entrances.

Bottom
of trench seen
here.

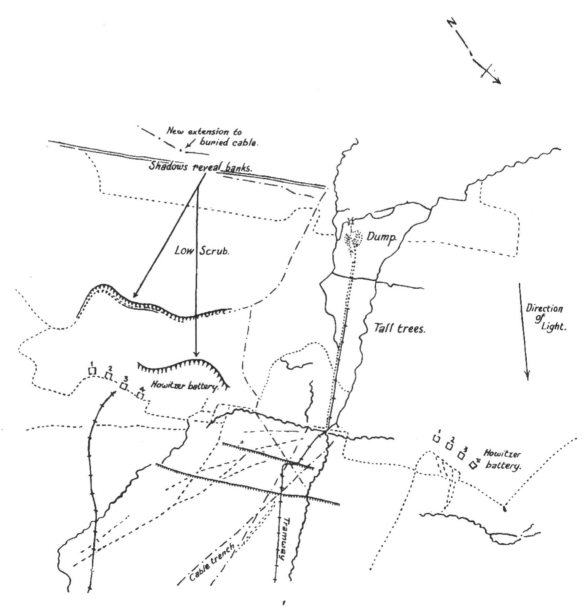

N

New extension to
buried cable.

Shadows reveal banks.

Low Scrub.

Dump.

Tall trees.

Direction of Light.

1 2
3 4 Howitzer battery.

1 2
3
4 Howitzer battery.

Cable trench

Tramway

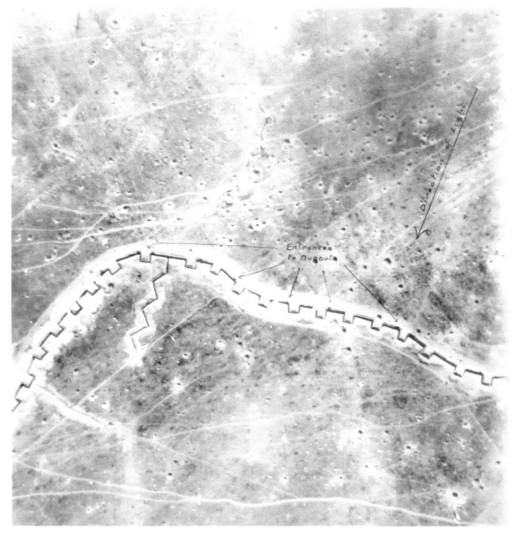

PLATE 5.

PHOTOGRAPHS CORRECTLY AND
INCORRECTLY MARKED.

Photograph correctly marked

Photograph incorrectly marked.

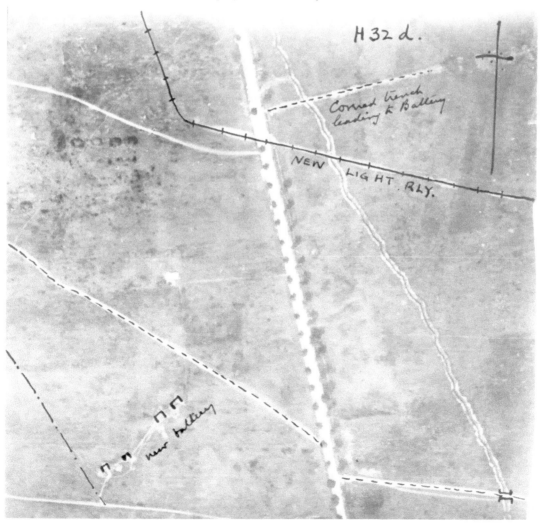

PLATE 6.

NEW PHOTOGRAPH SHOWING
ALTERATION IN DETAIL OF
AN OLD CADASTRAL PLAN.

Recent Photograph showing alteration in detail of an old cadastral plan.
At "A" the by-road has been straightened and now becomes the main road, while
at "B" what was the main road is now the by-road.

PLATE 7.

METHOD OF TRANSFERRING DETAIL
RAPIDLY AND ACCURATELY FROM A
PHOTOGRAPH TO A MAP.

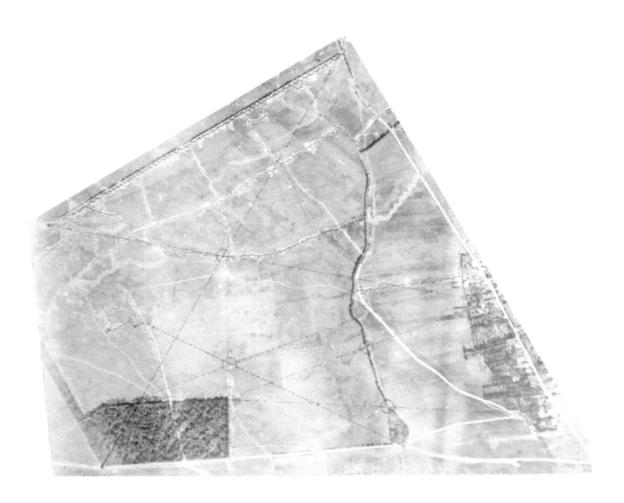

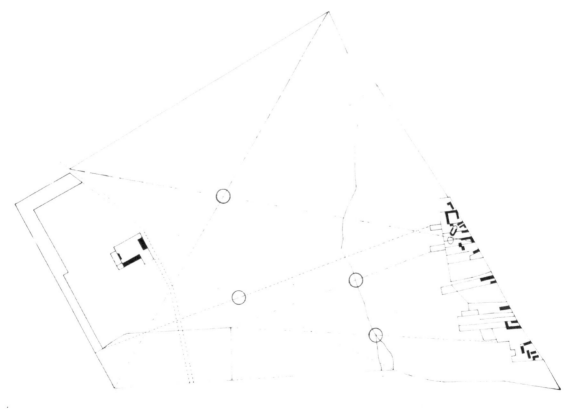

METHOD OF TRANSFERRING DETAIL RAPIDLY
AND ACCURATELY FROM A PHOTOGRAPH TO A MAP.

On the photograph, select four points easily identified on the map, which are so situated that the lines joining them intersect on or close to the particular detail which it is desired to fix.

On the map, draw lines joining the corresponding points; the intersection of these lines will give the true position of the particular detail in question.

The remainder of the detail can be quickly drawn in with the aid of proportional compasses.

It will be seen from the illustration that three trench junctions and the corner of the small wood have been determined by this method.

PLATE 8.

MODEL OF A TYPICAL TRENCH
MORTAR EMPLACEMENT.

MODEL OF A TYPICAL TRENCH MORTAR EMPLACEMENT.

The model was made before the salvage parties had removed the trench mortar and ammunition.

Time taken about 30 minutes.

Materials an old cigarette tin, a wooden match box and a few handfuls of cement.

The model was dusted with table salt before being photographed, in order to give the appearance of earth as shown on a photograph.

Copies and a description of the photograph were immediately sent to Corps, to compare with emplacements of similar appearance opposite their front.

Photographed from above.

Photographed from the entrance end.

PLATE 9.

MACHINE GUN EMPLACEMENTS.

*AREA :—*La Bassée Canal to River Scarpe.

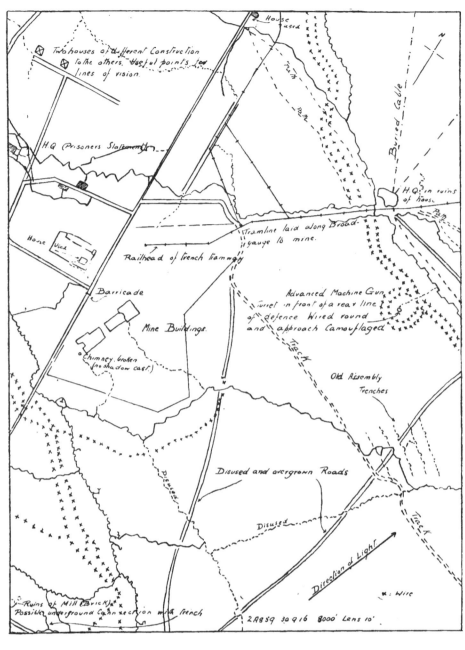

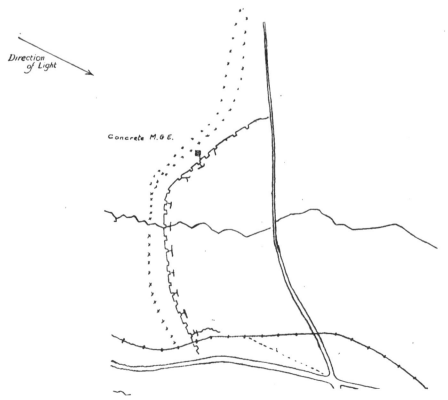

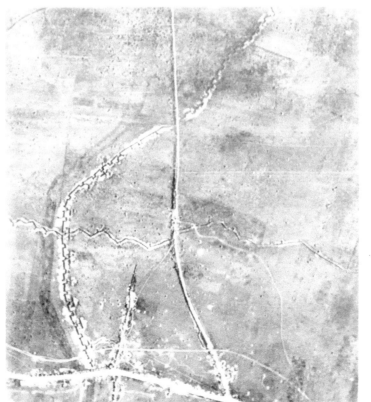

PLATE 10.

MACHINE GUN EMPLACEMENTS.

AREA :—La Bassée Canal to River Scarpe.

River Ancre to River Somme.

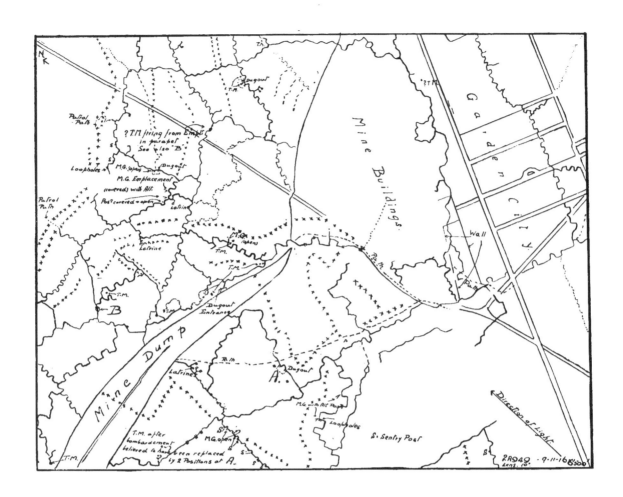

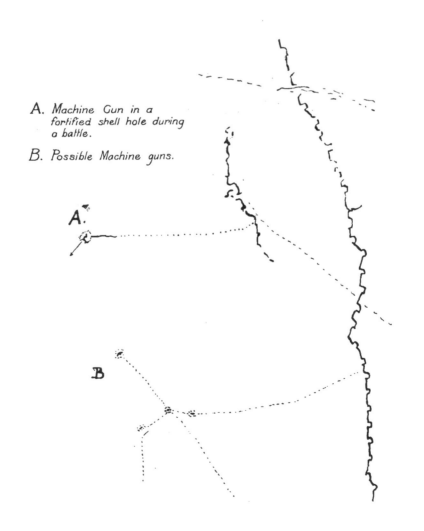

A. Machine Gun in a fortified shell hole during a battle.

B. Possible Machine guns.

PLATE 11.

TRENCH MORTAR EMPLACEMENTS.

AREA :—River Scarpe to River Ancre.
La Bassée Canal to River Scarpe.

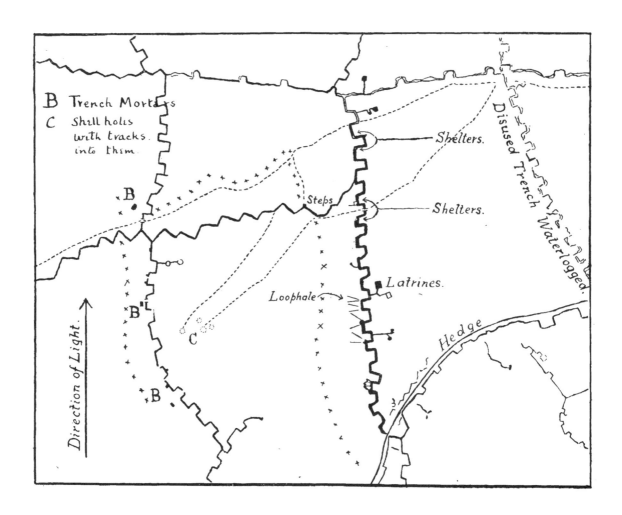

B Trench Mortars
C Shell holes with tracks into them.

Direction of Light

Shelters.

Steps

Shelters.

Loophole

Latrines.

Disused Trench Waterlogged.

Hedge

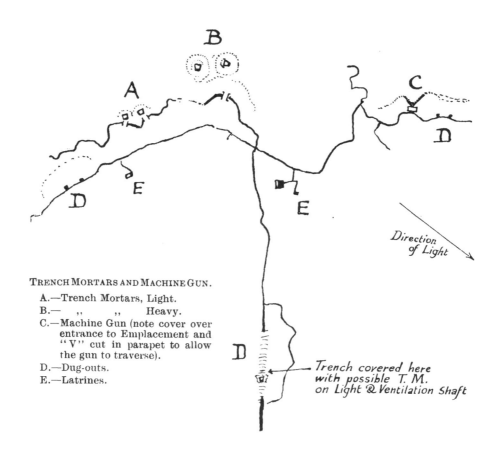

B

A

C

D

D

E

E

Direction of Light

TRENCH MORTARS AND MACHINE GUN.

A.—Trench Mortars, Light.
B.—   ,,   ,,   Heavy.
C.—Machine Gun (note cover over entrance to Emplacement and "V" cut in parapet to allow the gun to traverse).
D.—Dug-outs.
E.—Latrines.

D

Trench covered here with possible T. M. on Light & Ventilation Shaft

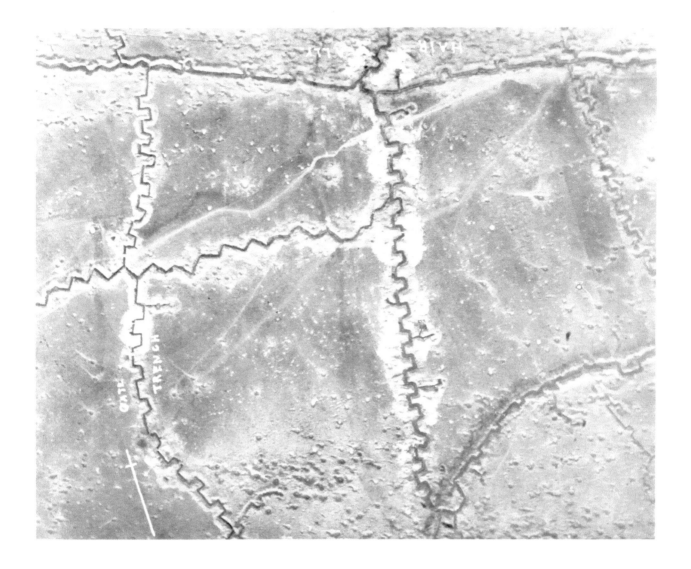

PLATE 12.

OBLIQUE PHOTOGRAPHS SHOWING
MACHINE GUN AND TRENCH MORTAR
EMPLACEMENTS.

AREA :—River Scarpe to River Ancre.

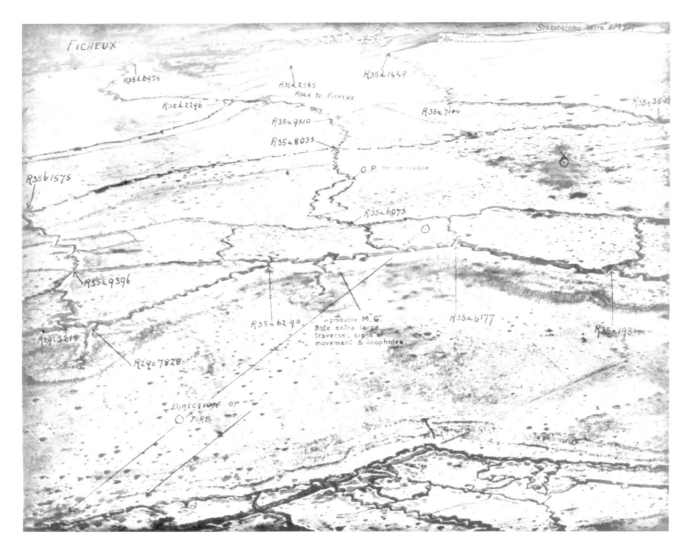

FICHEUX

R35b6958
R35b2296
R35a2565
Road to Ficheux
R35a1449
R35e7140
R35a35
R35a9510
R35a8035
O.P. for periscope
R35b1575
R35a6073
R35b9396
R35a6290
probable M.G.
Note extra large
traverse, signs of
movement & loopholes
R35ab177
R35a1981
R29c5218
R29c7828
DIRECTION OF
⊙ FIRE
STEREOSCOPIC WITH H.M.507

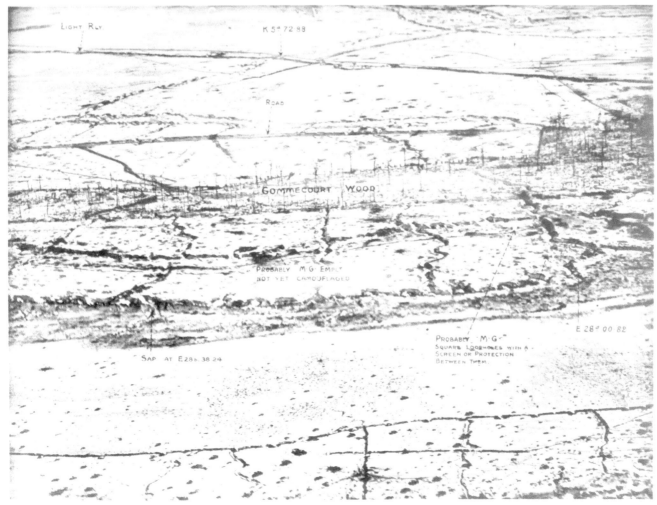

LIGHT RLY.
K5a72.88
ROAD
GOMMECOURT WOOD
PROBABLY M.G. EMPLT
NOT YET CAMOUFLAGED
PROBABLY M.G.
SQUARE LOOPHOLES WITH A
SCREEN OR PROTECTION
BETWEEN THEM.
E28d00.82
SAP AT E28b.38.24

PLATE 13.

NORMAL TYPES OF BATTERY EMPLACEMENT.

BATTERY IN HOUSES.
BATTERIES IN A WOOD.

AREA : – La Bassée Canal to River Scarpe.

River Scarpe to River Ancre.

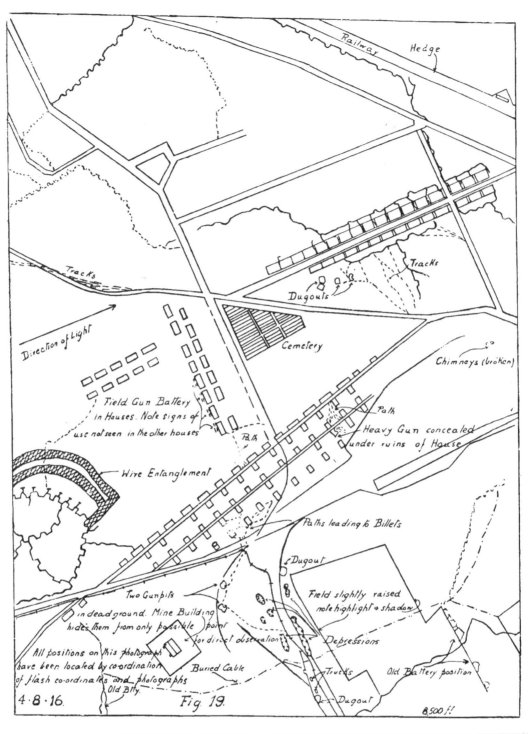

Railway

Hedge

Tracks

Dugouts

Tracks

Direction of Light

Cemetery

Chimneys (broken)

Field Gun Battery
in Houses. Note signs of
use not seen in the other houses

Path

Heavy Gun concealed
under ruins of House

Path

Wire Entanglement

Paths leading to Billets

Dugout

Two Gunpits
in dead ground. Mine Building
hides them from only possible point
for direct observation

Field slightly raised
note highlight & shadow

Depressions

All positions on this photograph
have been located by coordination
of flash co-ordinates and photographs
Old Bty.

Trucks

Old Battery position

Buried Cable

Dugout

4·8·16.

Fig. 19.

8,500 ft.

Direction
of Light

A.

B.

AT A. A GUN BATTERY. AT B. A HOWITZER BATTERY
THE FLAT TRAJECTORY GUNS HAVE MADE FOUR CLEAR
BLAST MARKS. THE HOWITZERS ARE FURTHER IN. NO
BLAST MARKS ARE APPARENT, BUT THE LEAVES
AND SMALL BRANCHES HAVE BEEN BLOWN AWAY
AT THE EDGE OF THE WOOD.

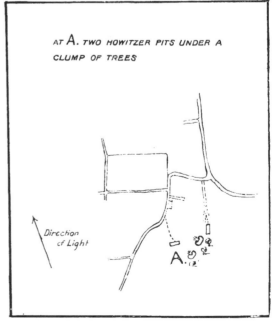

AT A. TWO HOWITZER PITS UNDER A
CLUMP OF TREES

Direction
of Light

A.

PLATE 14.

BATTERY IN OPEN COUNTRY.
BATTERY IN COTTAGE RUINS.

AREA :—Boesinghe to Ypres-Comines Canal.
La Bassée Canal to River Scarpe.

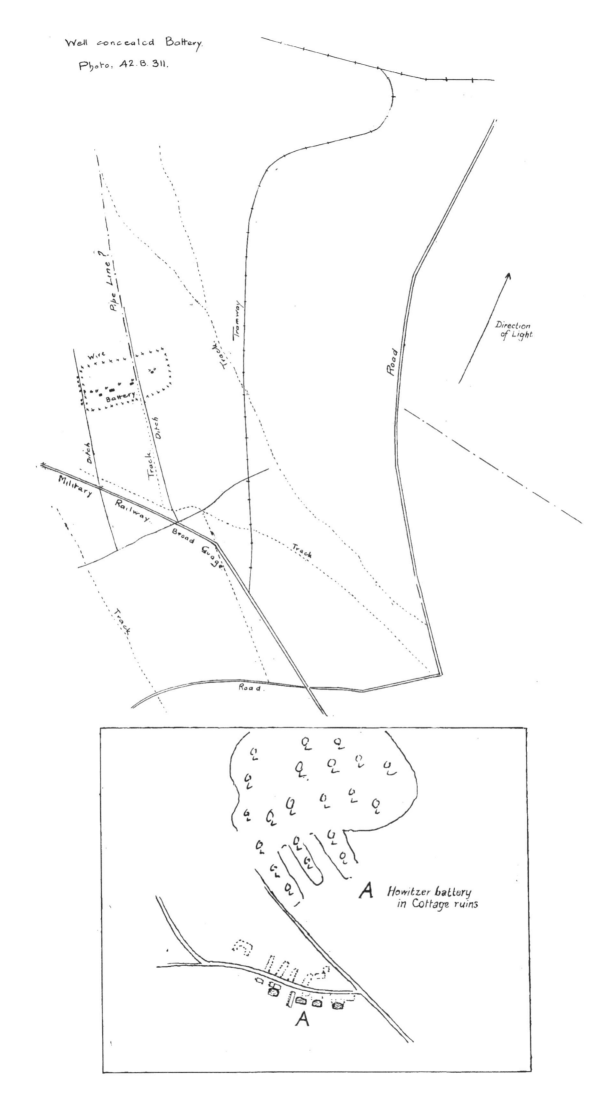

Well concealed Battery.

Photo, 42.B.311.

Pipe Line?

Track

Tramway

Wire

Battery

Road

Direction
of Light.

Ditch

Track

Ditch

Military

Railway

Broad Guage

Track

Road.

Track

A   Howitzer battery
in Cottage ruins

A

PLATE 15.

HOWITZER PITS IN AN ORCHARD.
TRENCH EMPLACEMENTS.

AREA :—River Ancre to River Somme.

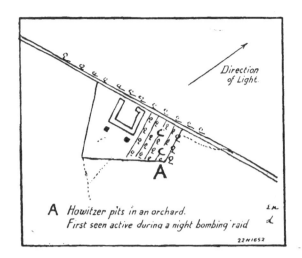

A Howitzer pits in an orchard.
First seen active during a night bombing raid

Direction of Light.

22 N 1652

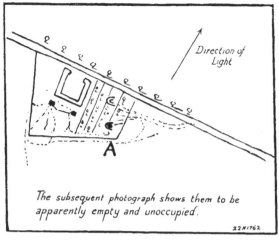

Direction of Light

The subsequent photograph shows them to be
apparently empty and unoccupied.

22 N 1762

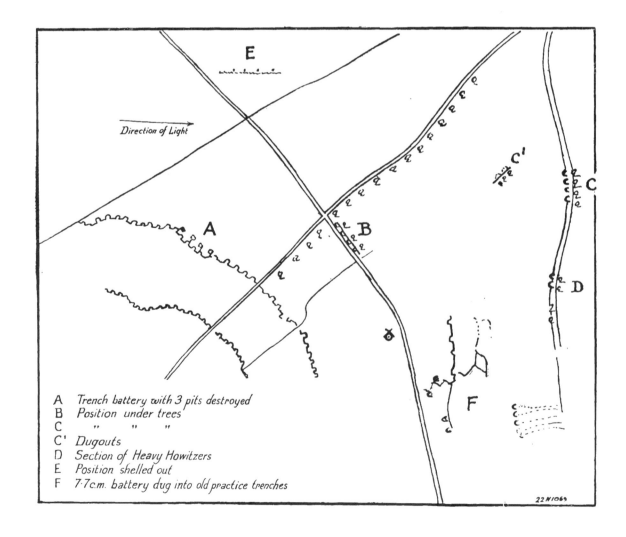

E

Direction of Light

C'

C

A

B

D

F

A   Trench battery with 3 pits destroyed
B   Position under trees
C   "   "   "
C' Dugouts
D   Section of Heavy Howitzers
E   Position shelled out
F   7·7 c.m. battery dug into old practice trenches

22 N 1069

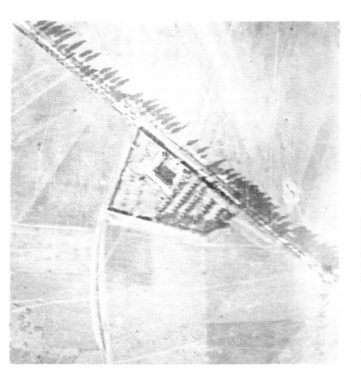

PLATE 16.

TRENCH EMPLACEMENT.
BATTERY DUG INTO A ROAD BANK.
GUNS FIRING UNDER CAMOUFLAGE
FROM THE OPEN.

AREA :—River Ancre to River Somme.

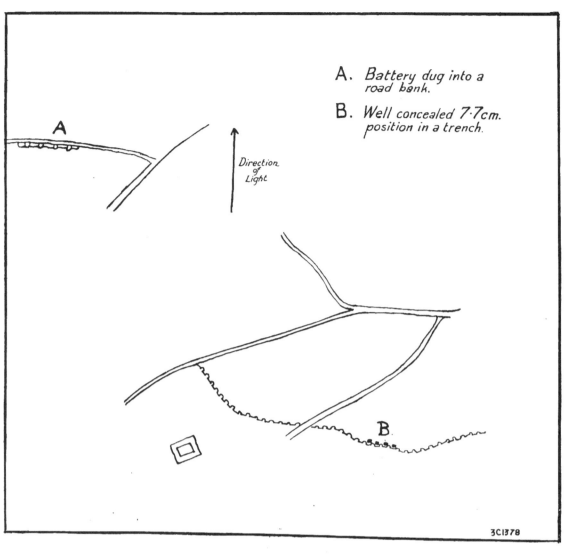

A. Battery dug into a
   road bank.

B. Well concealed 7·7cm.
   position in a trench.

Direction
of
Light

3C1378

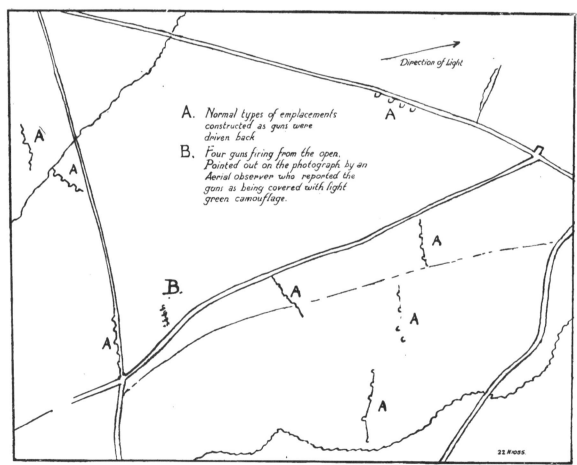

Direction of Light

A. Normal types of emplacements
   constructed as guns were
   driven back

B. Four guns firing from the open.
   Pointed out on the photograph by an
   Aerial observer who reported the
   guns as being covered with light
   green camouflage.

22 N1055.

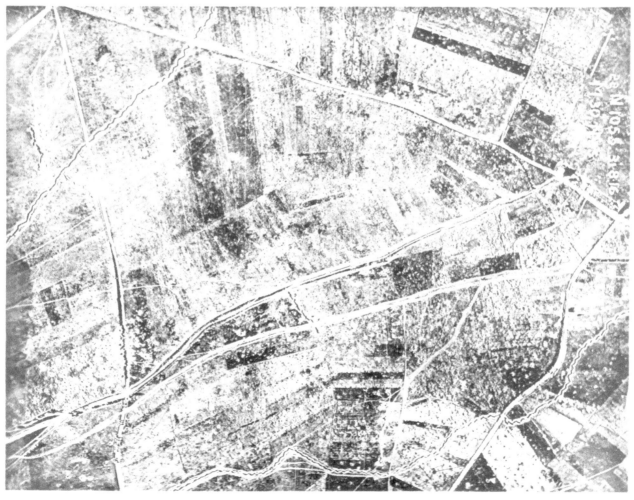

PLATE 17.

DUMMY EMPLACEMENT.
ANTI-AIRCRAFT EMPLACEMENT.

AREA :—River Ancre to River Somme.
La Bassée Canal to River Scarpe.

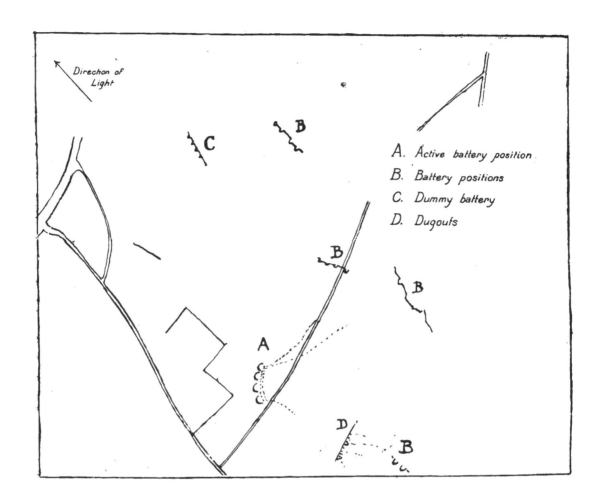

Direction of Light

A. Active battery position.
B. Battery positions
C. Dummy battery
D. Dugouts

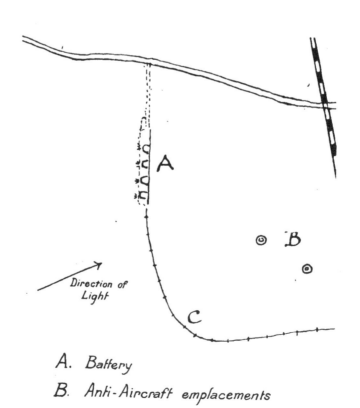

Direction of Light

A. Battery
B. Anti-Aircraft emplacements
C. 40 cm. tramway

13L307

PLATE 18.

DUMMY EMPLACEMENTS.

AREA .—River Scarpe to River Ancre.
    La Bassée Canal to River Scarpe.
    River Scarpe to River Ancre.

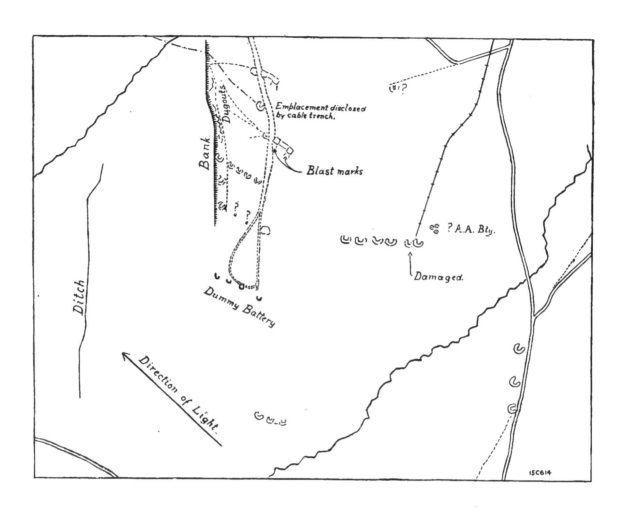

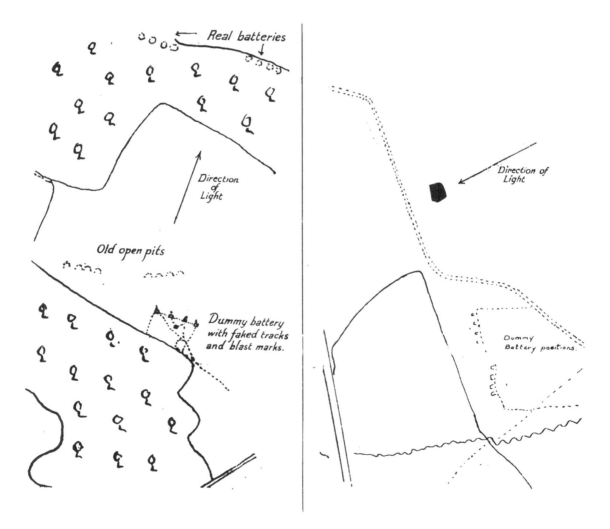

Dummy
Battery   1.
Positions.

2.

PLATE 19.

ABNORMAL TYPES OF BATTERY EMPLACEMENT.

HOWITZER BATTERY DUG-IN. •
EMPLACEMENT TUNNELLED UNDER A RAILWAY EMBANKMENT.
"A PIECES."

AREA :—River Scarpe to River Ancre.

A.—Howitzer battery dug-in.
B.—Wire.

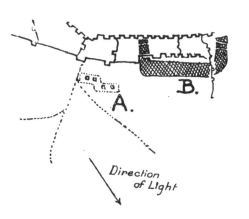

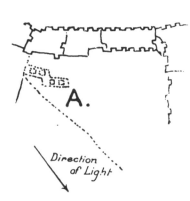

A. same battery camouflaged

EMPLACEMENT TUNNELLED UNDER A
RAILWAY EMBANKMENT.
    A.—Entrances.
    B.—Ports.

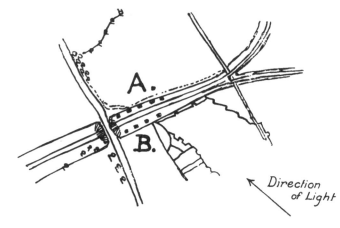

OBLIQUE PHOTOGRAPH OF ABOVE.
  B.—Ports.

The embankment is very high.   Compare
with houses in the foreground.

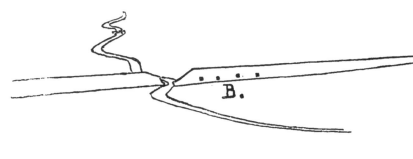

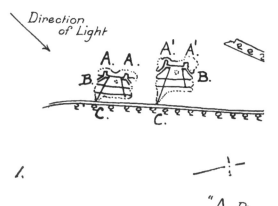

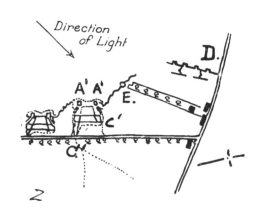

"A Pieces"

1. A.A.—Gun-pits uncovered.
      B.—Ramp to run guns in.
      C.—Inclined trench from road.

2. Northern "A Piece" occupied.
    A'.A'.—Covered pits.
    C'.C'.—Tracks where guns have been run-
         in and ammunition brought up.
      D.—"Aeroplane" emplacement.
      E.—Battery commander's dug-out.

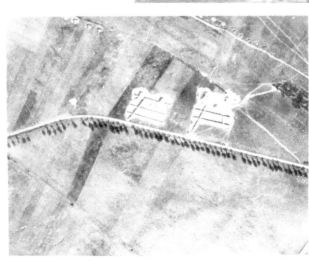

PLATE 20.

HEAVY GUN POSITION.

AREA :—Ypres-Comines Canal to La Bassée Canal.

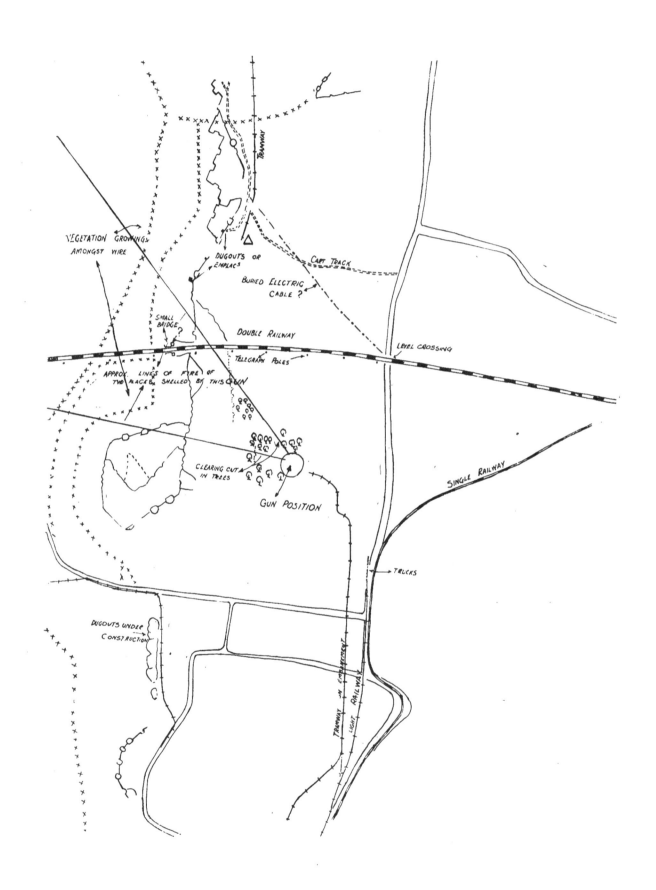

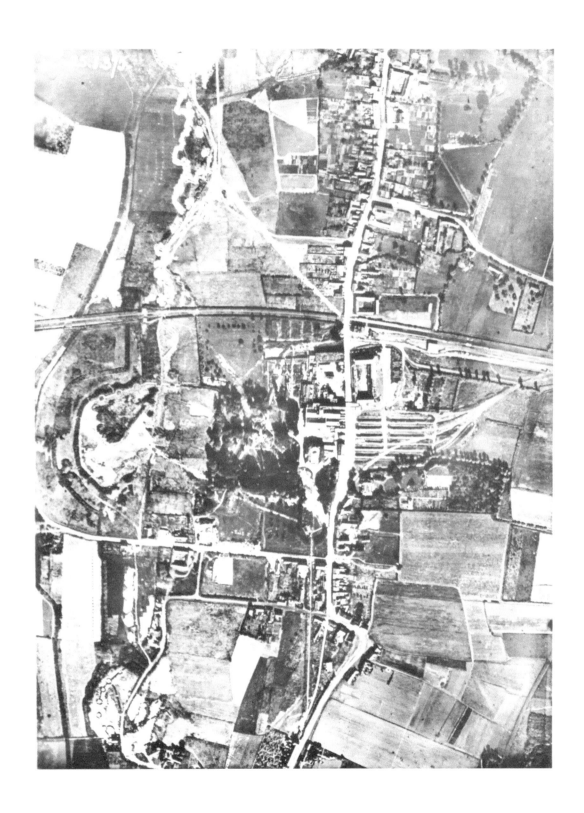

PLATE 21.

"AEROPLANE" EMPLACEMENTS.
HEAVY HOWITZER PITS.
EMPLACEMENT UNDER CONSTRUCTION.

AREA :—River Scarpe to River Ancre.

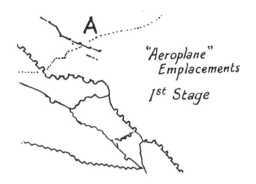

"Aeroplane" Emplacements 1st Stage

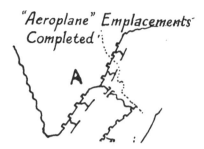

"Aeroplane" Emplacements Completed

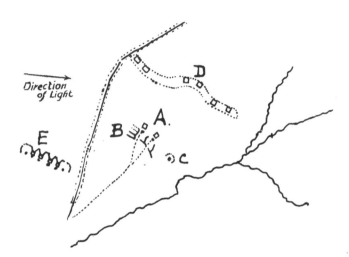

Direction of Light

A.—Emplacement for heavy Howitzers.

B.—Trenches for men and ammunition.

C.—Battery commander's dug-out.

D.—Six-gun battery in an artificial bank.

E.—Emplacement with heavy cover cut away in " V "'s in front of the pits.

EMPLACEMENT UNDER CONSTRUCTION.

1. A.—First trench dug.

    B.—Entrances to dug-outs under the road.

2. A.—3 pits covered, 1 still uncovered.

    B.—Dug-outs further advanced.

3. Pits covered over and dug-outs camouflaged.

4. A A A A.—Blast marks.

    B.—Covered trench leading to communication trench.

    The road has been continued over and through the emplacement to prevent signs of use up to, but not beyond, the battery.

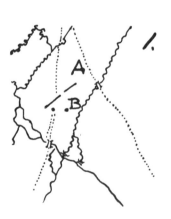

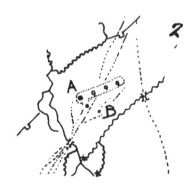

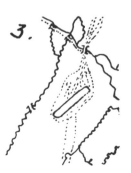

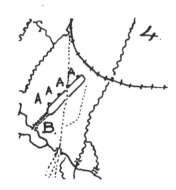

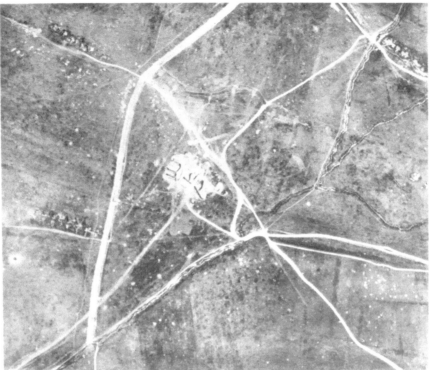

Emplacement under construction.

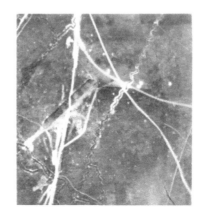

PLATE 22.

GUNS FIRING.

BLAST MARKS IN SNOW.

AREA :—River Scarpe to River Ancre.

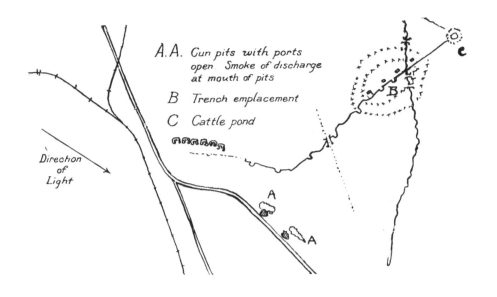

A.A. Gun pits with ports open. Smoke of discharge at mouth of pits

B Trench emplacement

C Cattle pond

Direction of Light

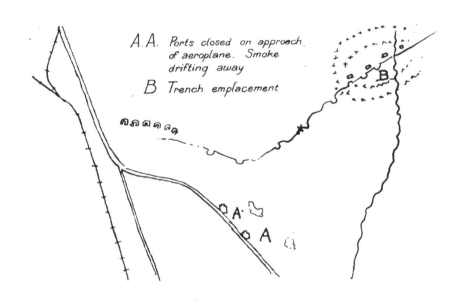

A.A. Ports closed on approach of aeroplane. Smoke drifting away

B Trench emplacement

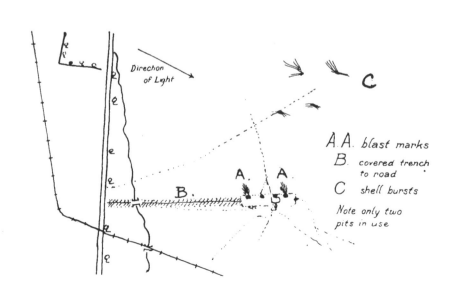

Direction of Light

A.A. blast marks

B covered trench to road

C shell bursts

Note only two pits in use

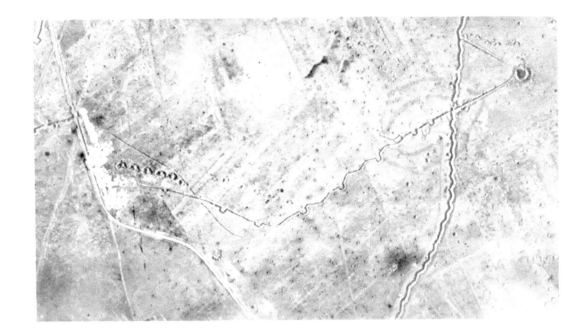

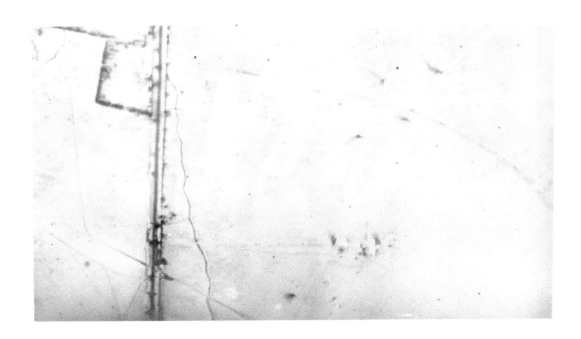

PLATE 23.

NORMAL GAUGE RAILWAY.

LIGHT RAILWAY.

*AREA :—*River Scarpe to River Ancre.

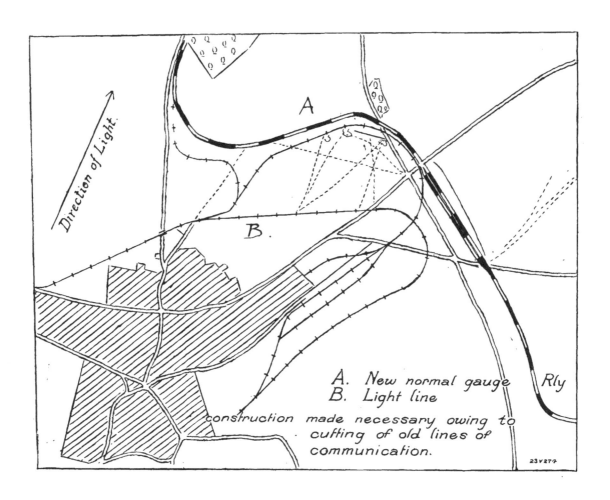

Direction of Light.

A

B.

A. New normal gauge Rly
B. Light line

construction made necessary owing to
cutting of old lines of
communication.

23 v 27.

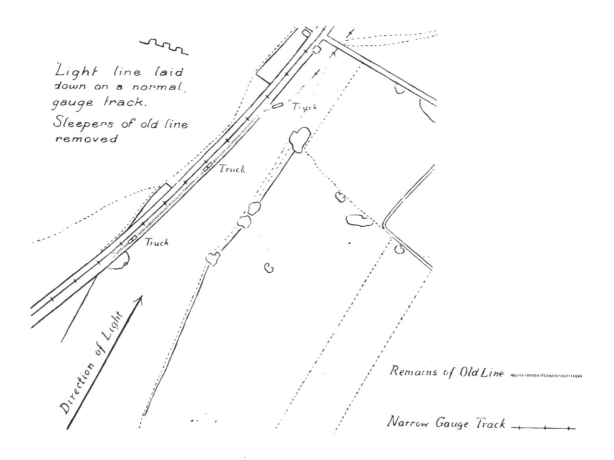

Light line laid
down on a normal.
gauge track.

Sleepers of old line
removed

Truck

Truck

Truck

Direction of Light

Remains of Old Line ▬▬▬▬▬▬▬▬▬▬▬

Narrow Gauge Track —+——+——+—

TRENCH TRAMWAY.

0·60 M. LIGHT RAILWAY. TRACKS.

AREA :—La Bassée Canal to River Scarpe.
River Scarpe to River Ancre.

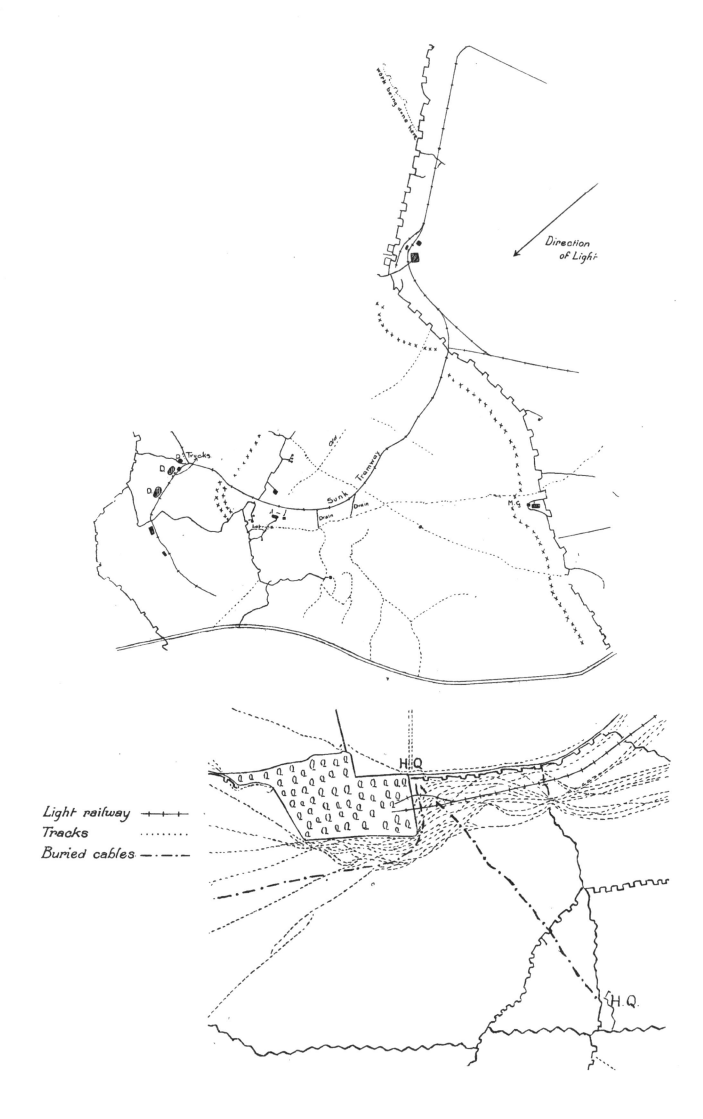

Direction
of Light

Sunk Tramway

Old

Drain   Drain

D. Trucks

D.

D.

M.G.

H.Q.

H.Q.

Light railway +++
Tracks ⋯⋯⋯
Buried cables —·—·—

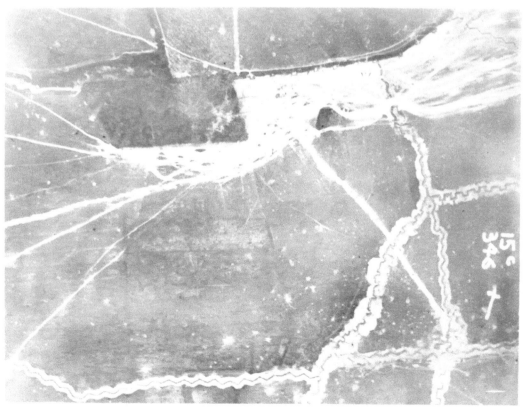

PLATE 25.

BURIED CABLES.

AREA :—Ypres—Comines Canal to La Bassée Canal.

La Bassée Canal to River Scarpe.

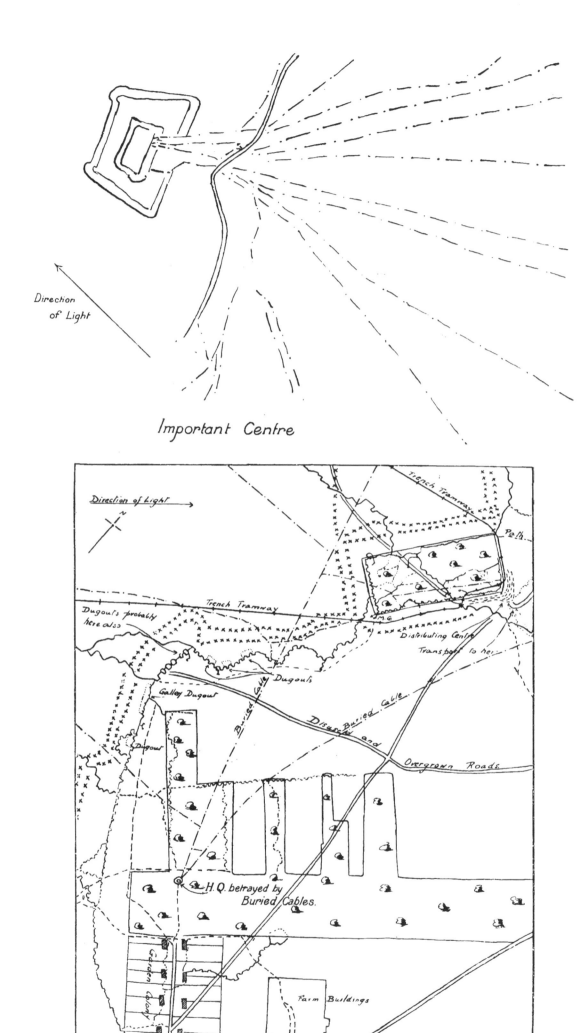

Direction
of Light

Important Centre

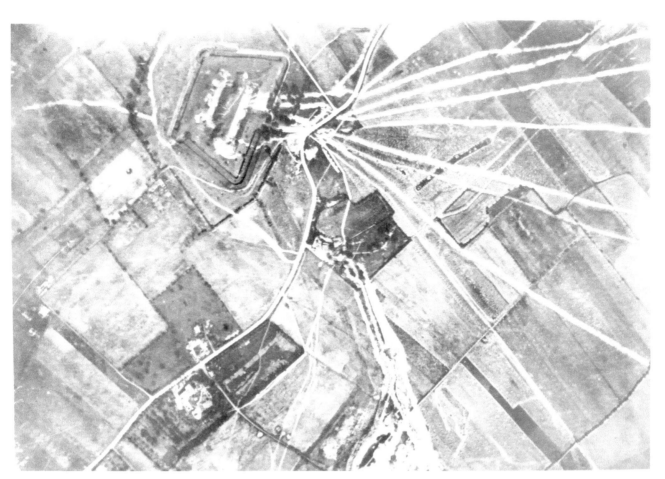

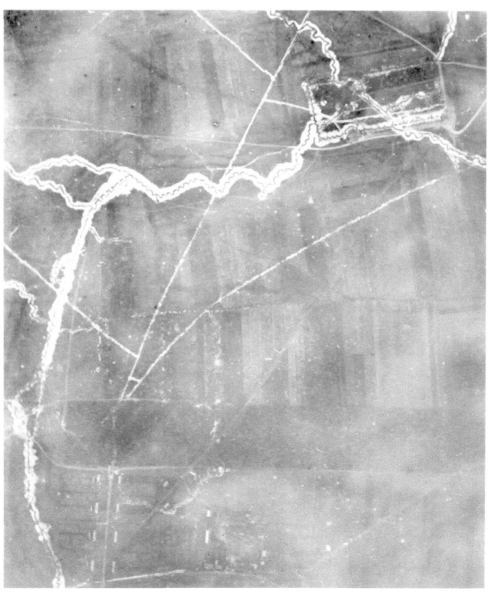

PLATE 26.

AIR LINES.

AREA :—River Scarpe to River Ancre.

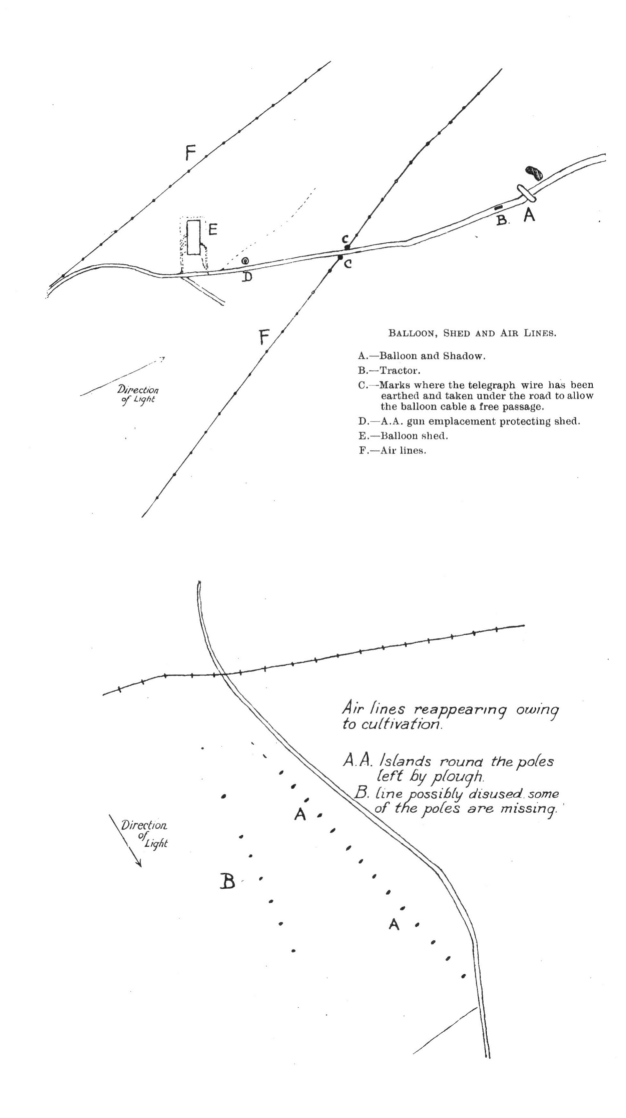

F

F

E

D

C
C

B. A

Direction of Light

BALLOON, SHED AND AIR LINES.

A.—Balloon and Shadow.

B.—Tractor.

C.—Marks where the telegraph wire has been earthed and taken under the road to allow the balloon cable a free passage.

D.—A.A. gun emplacement protecting shed.

E.—Balloon shed.

F.—Air lines.

Air lines reappearing owing to cultivation.

A.A. Islands round the poles left by plough.

B. line possibly disused some of the poles are missing.

A

B

A

Direction of Light

PLATE 27.

DUG-OUTS.

AREA :—River Scarpe to River Ancre.

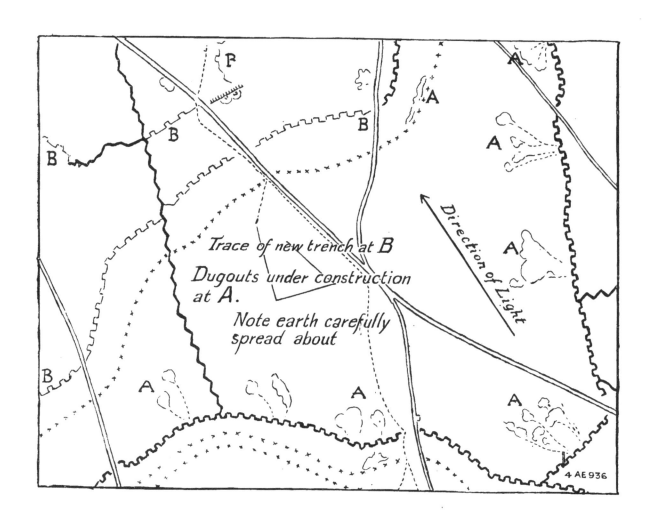

Trace of new trench at B

Dugouts under construction at A.

Note earth carefully spread about

Direction of Light

4 AE 936

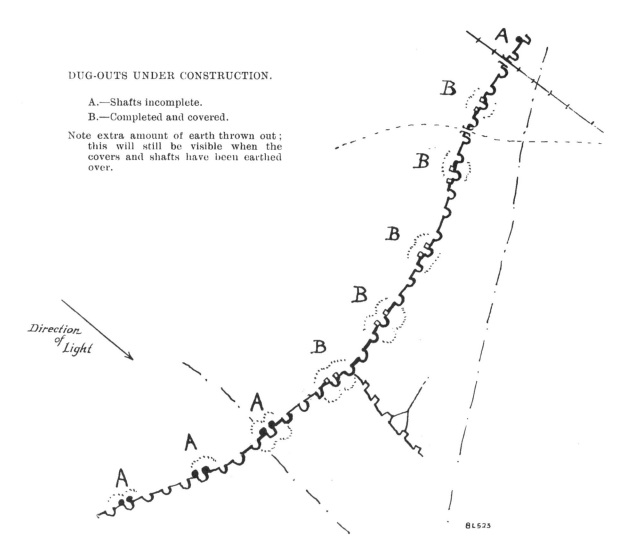

DUG-OUTS UNDER CONSTRUCTION.

A.—Shafts incomplete.
B.—Completed and covered.

Note extra amount of earth thrown out ;
this will still be visible when the
covers and shafts have been earthed
over.

Direction of Light

8L523

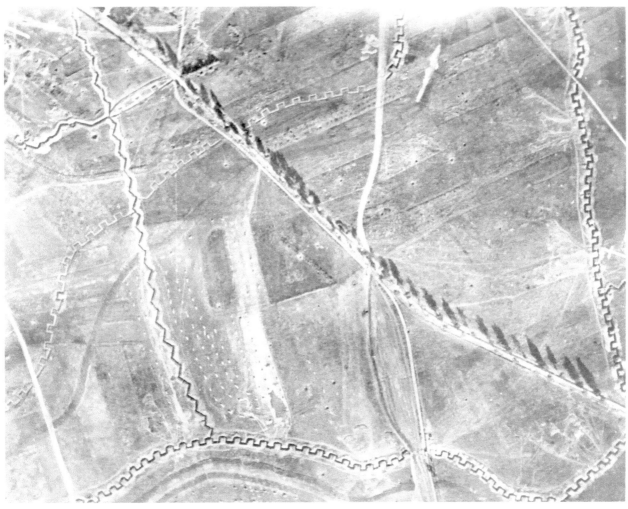

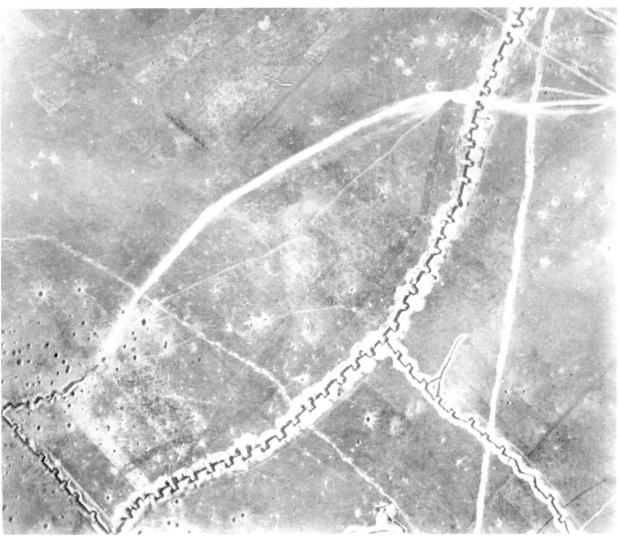

PLATE 28.

MINE SHAFTS.

AREA:—La Bassée Canal to River Scarpe.

N

Former Tramline
now removed

Dugout

M.G.

Quarries

Disused

Latrine

Latrine

Path

Latrine

Loopholes

Open M.G.

M.G.
Covered

S

S

S

T.M.

Probable Entrances to
Galleries leading to a Mine
Shaft.

Mine Craters fortified
and firestepped.

Direction of Light

S = Sentry Post.
xxx = Wire

25.v.i.646. 10.10.16.

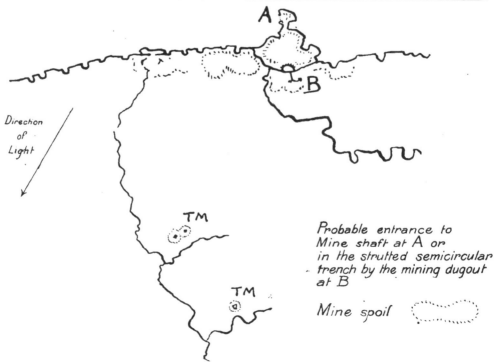

A

B

Direction
of
Light

TM

TM

Probable entrance to
Mine shaft at A or
in the strutted semicircular
trench by the mining dugout
at B

Mine spoil

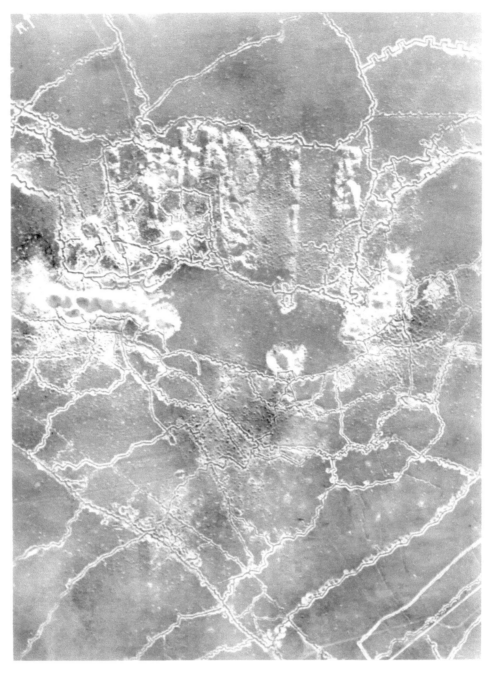

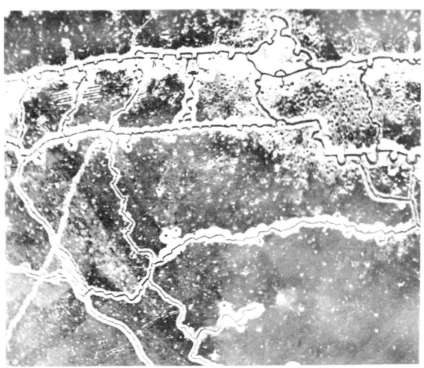

PLATE 29.

FORTIFIED CRATERS.
TYPICAL STRONG POINT.

AREA :—Ypres-Comines Canal to La Bassée Canal.
River Scarpe to River Ancre.

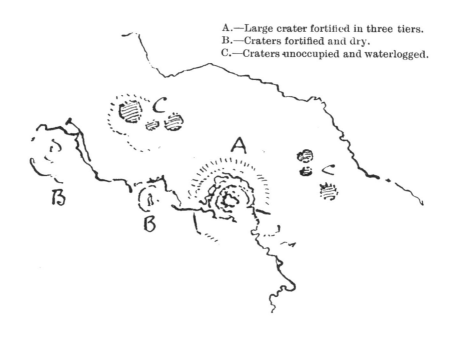

A.—Large crater fortified in three tiers.
B.—Craters fortified and dry.
C.—Craters unoccupied and waterlogged.

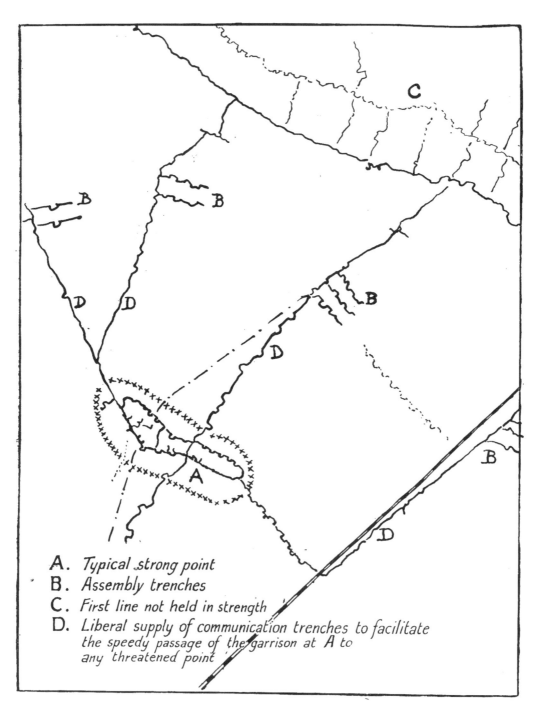

A. Typical strong point
B. Assembly trenches
C. First line not held in strength
D. Liberal supply of communication trenches to facilitate the speedy passage of the garrison at A to any threatened point

PLATE 30.

BREASTWORKS.
ADVANCED LISTENING POSTS.   TRACKS.

AREA :—Ypres-Comines Canal to La Bassée Canal.
River Scarpe to River Ancre.

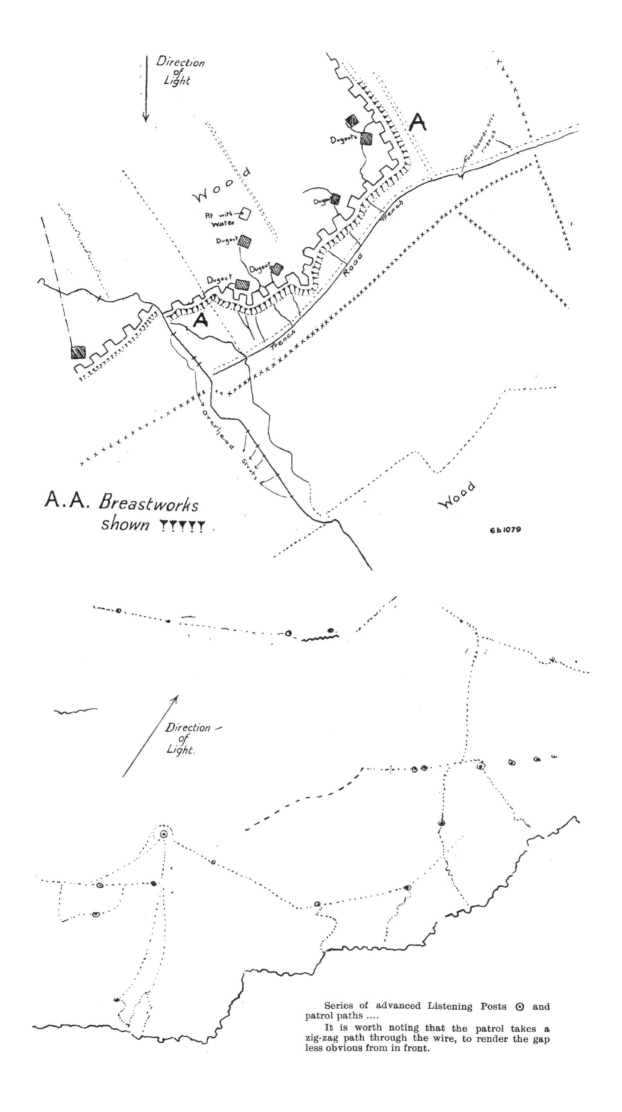

Direction
of
Light

Wood

A

Dugouts

Dugout

Dugout

Pit with
water

Dugout

Dugout

Trench

Road

Trench

Foot boards over
Trench

Trench

Overhead Struts

A

Wood

6 b 1079

A.A. Breastworks
shown ΥΥΥΥΥ

Direction —
of
Light.

Series of advanced Listening Posts ⊙ and
patrol paths ....
It is worth noting that the patrol takes a
zig-zag path through the wire, to render the gap
less obvious from in front.

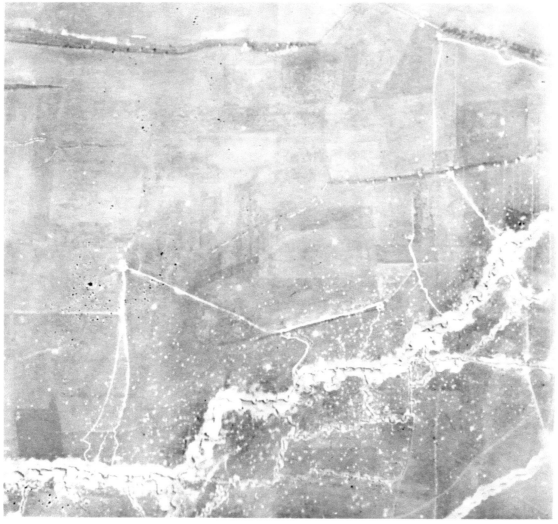

PLATE 31.

OBSERVATION POSTS.

AREA :—River Scarpe to River Ancre.

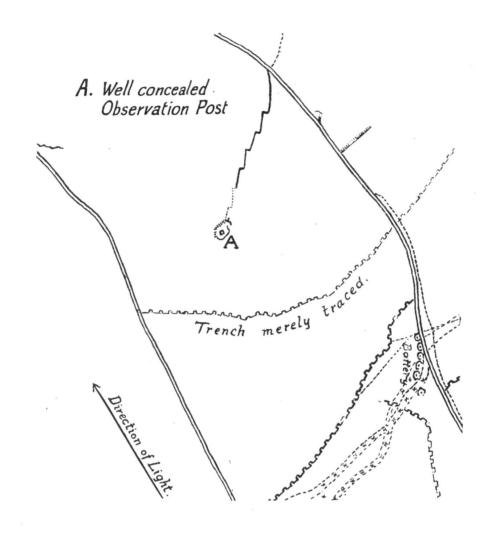

A. Well concealed Observation Post

Trench merely traced.

Direction of Light.

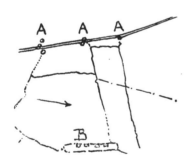

A.A.A.—Haystacks used as observation posts.

B.—Battery.

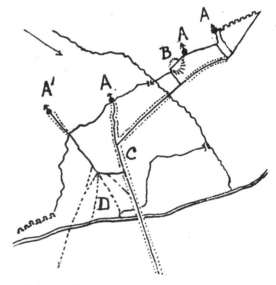

A.A.A.A.—Observation posts.

B.—Dug-out.

C.—Covered Trench for Cables and personnel.

D.—Tracks where observers have jumped into the trench just before reaching the sky line. These point to the observation post A´ being the most used.

Plate 32.

PREPARATION AGAINST ATTACK.

AREA :—River Ancre to River Somme.
La Bassée Canal to River Scarpe.

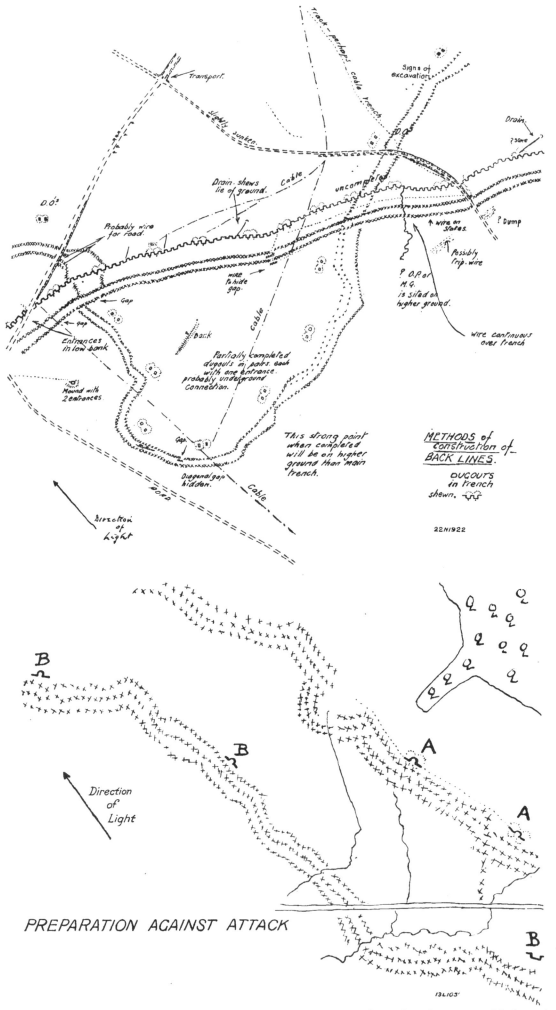

New lines of wire erected before the trench is dug. At A.A. trace of trench and traverses with dug-outs commenced. At B.B. traverses dug to mark course of new trench.

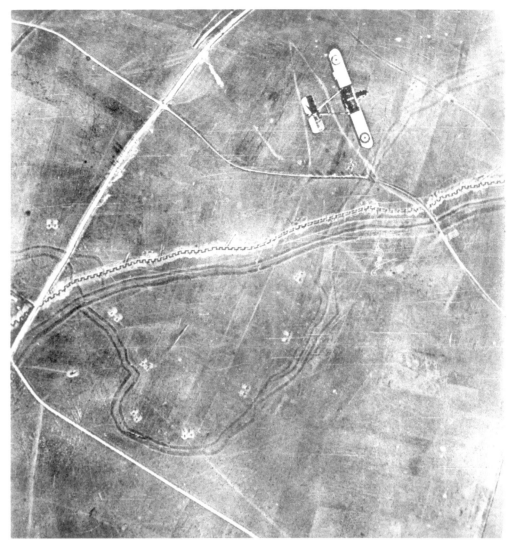

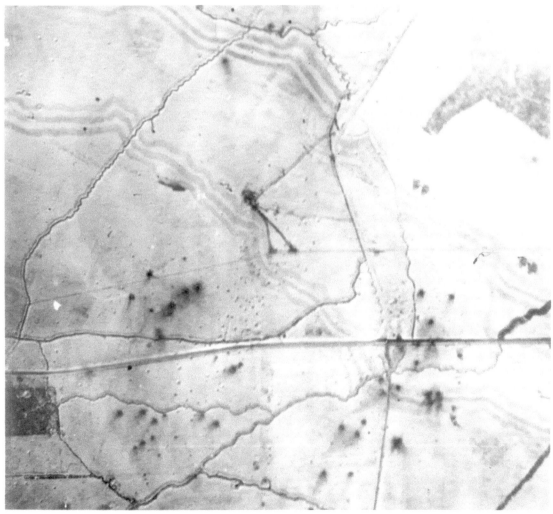

PLATE 33.

INDICATIONS OF A RAID OR AN ATTACK.

AREA :—La Bassée Canal to River Scarpe.

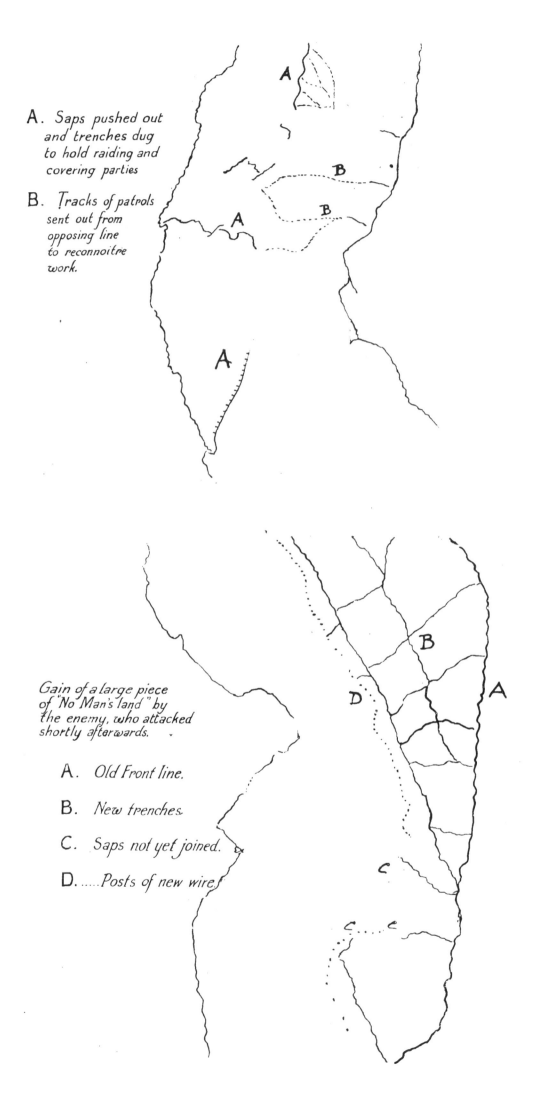

A. Saps pushed out
and trenches dug
to hold raiding and
covering parties

B. Tracks of patrols
sent out from
opposing line
to reconnoitre
work.

Gain of a large piece
of "No Man's land" by
the enemy, who attacked
shortly afterwards.

A. Old Front line.

B. New trenches.

C. Saps not yet joined.

D. .....Posts of new wire.

PLATE 34.

TRENCH CONSTRUCTION DURING A BATTLE.

BOMBING.   BLOCKS.

AREA :—River Ancre to River Somme.

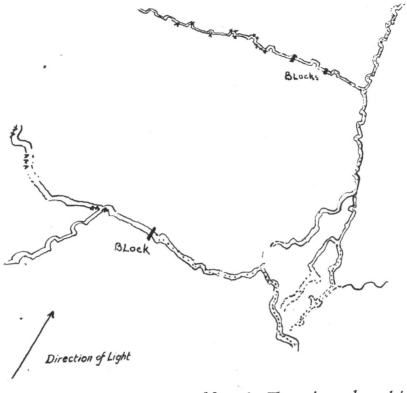

Blocks

Block

Direction of Light

Men in Trenches, bombing.

British.

Germans.

Track of further advance

Trench badly damaged by bombardment, but still held by us.

Direction of Light

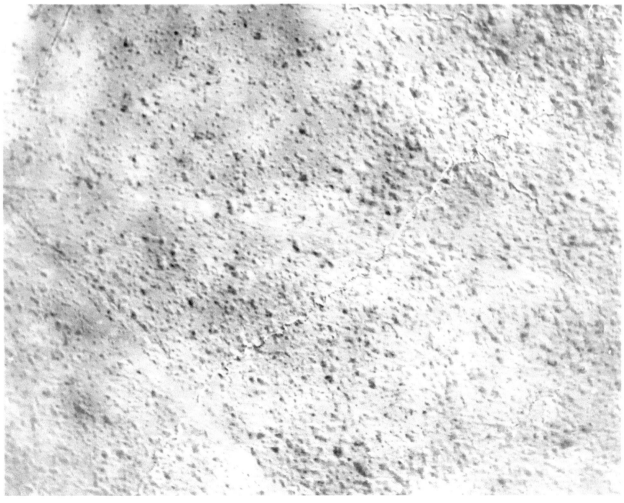

PLATE 35.

LINKING UP SHELL HOLES.

AREA :—River Ancre to River Somme.

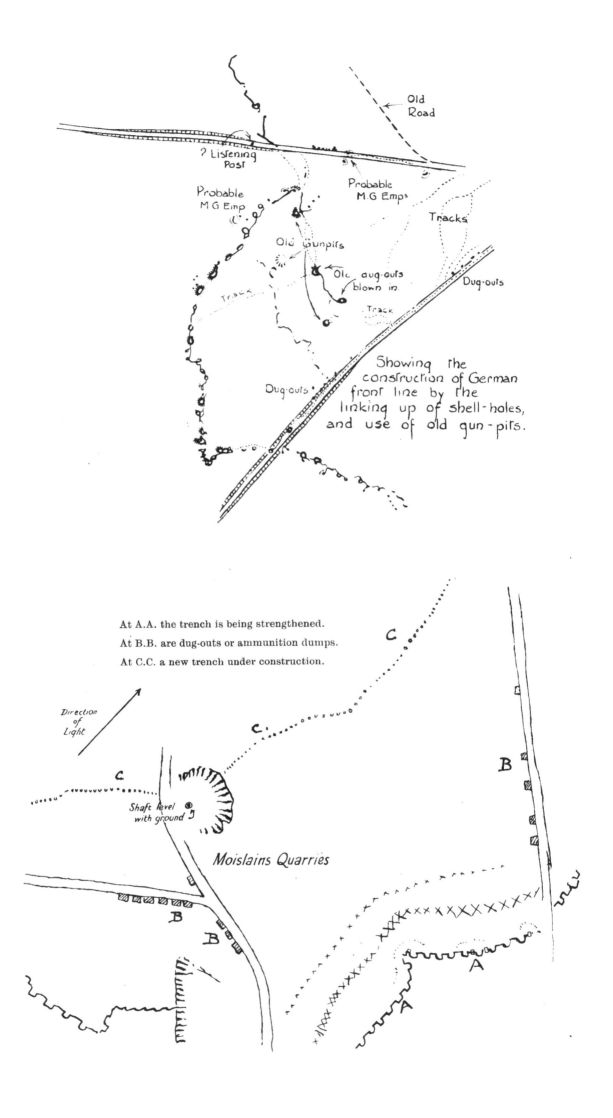

? Listening Post

Old Road

Probable M.G Emp

Probable M.G Emps

Tracks

Old Gunpits

Old dug-outs blown in.

Track

Dug-outs

Track

Dug-outs

Showing the construction of German front line by the linking up of shell-holes, and use of old gun-pits.

At A.A. the trench is being strengthened.

At B.B. are dug-outs or ammunition dumps.

At C.C. a new trench under construction.

C

C

C

Direction of Light

Shaft level with ground

Moislains Quarries

B

B

B

B

A

A

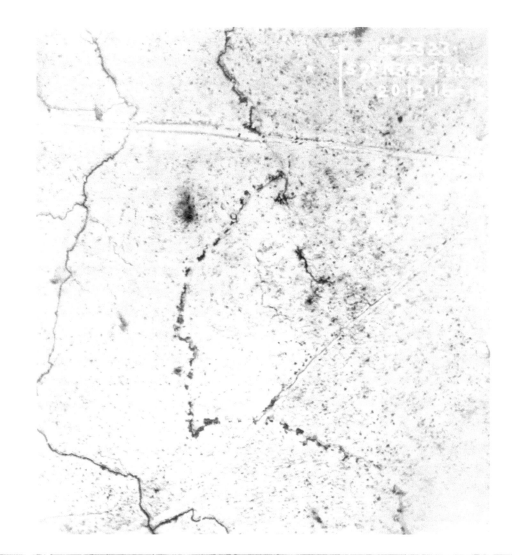

PLATE 36.

TRENCH BEFORE AND AFTER CAPTURE.

AREA :—River Ancre to River Somme.

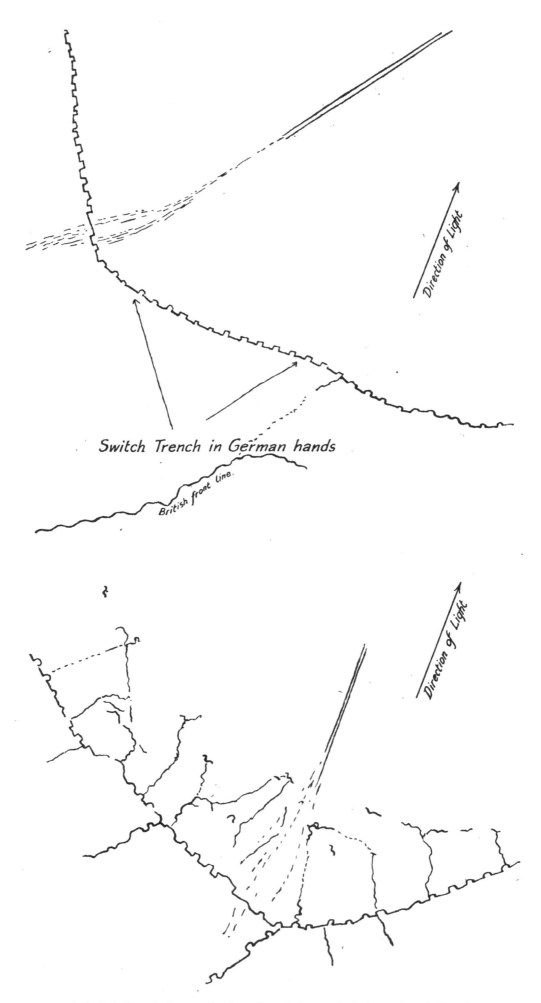

Switch Trench in our hands. Saps being pushed forward and linked up, preparatory to a further advance.

These photographs illustrate the importance of ascertaining the exact position of our troops.

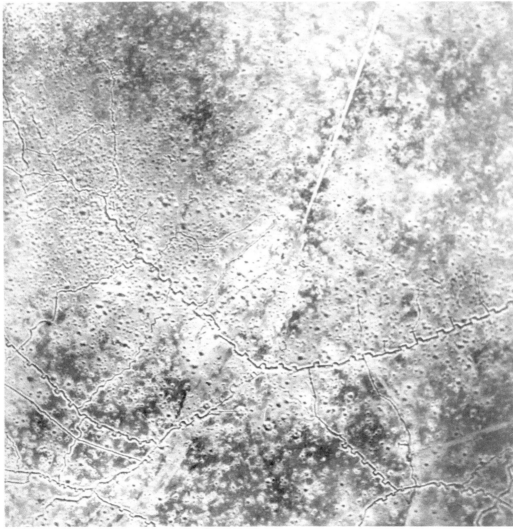

PLATE 37.

ADVANCED POST.
TRACKS.

AREA :—River Ancre to River Somme.

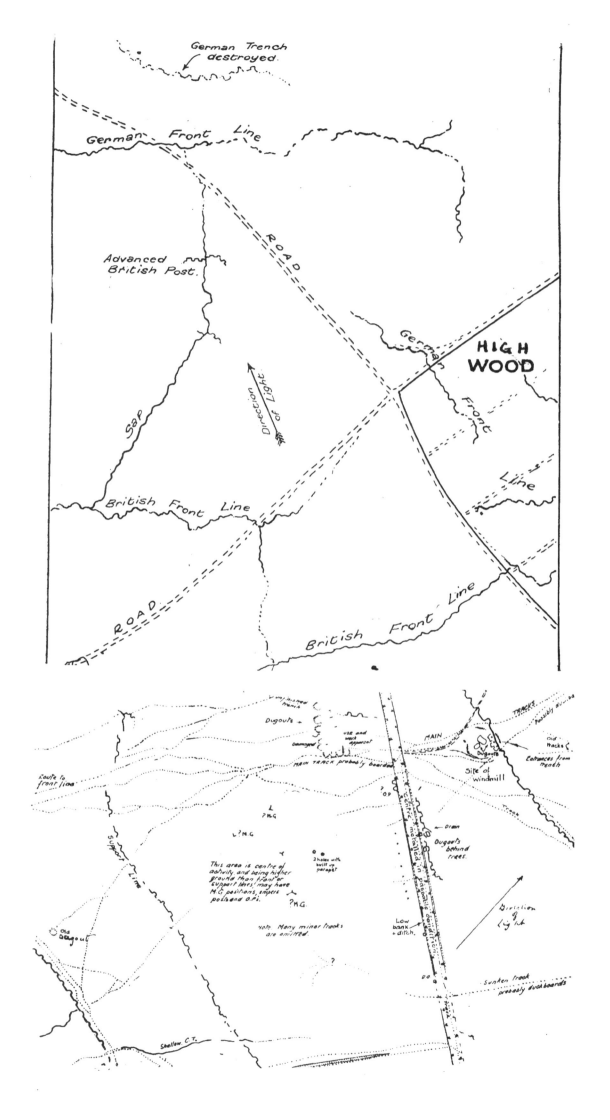

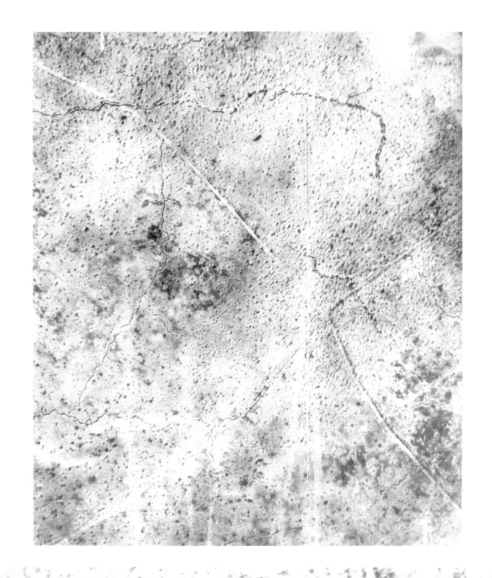

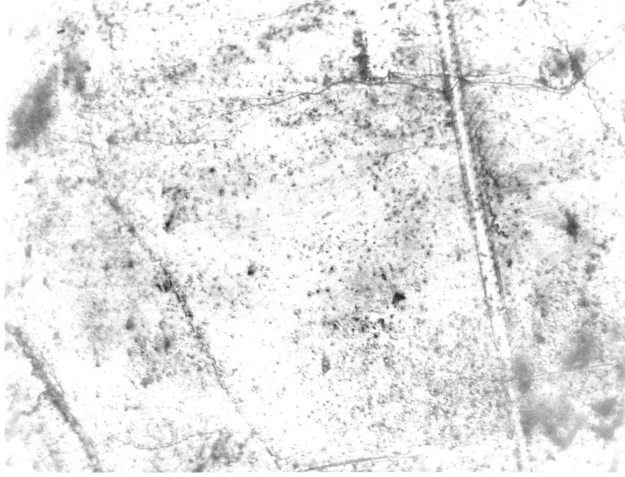

PLATE 38.

TRACKS.

AREA :—River Ancre to River Somme.

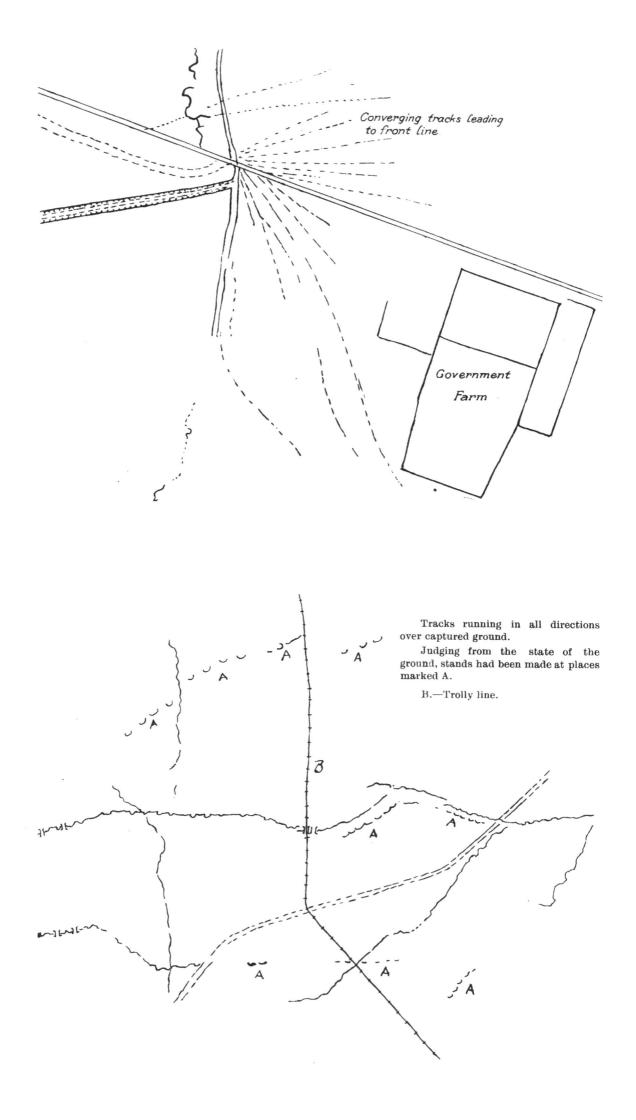

Converging tracks leading
to front line.

Government
Farm

Tracks running in all directions
over captured ground.

Judging from the state of the
ground, stands had been made at places
marked A.

B.—Trolly line.

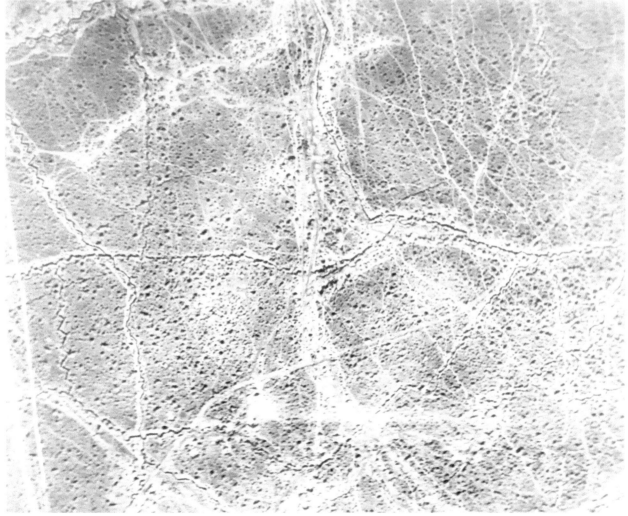

PLATE 39.

TANK TRAPS.

AREA :—River Scarpe to River Ancre.

River Ancre to River Somme.

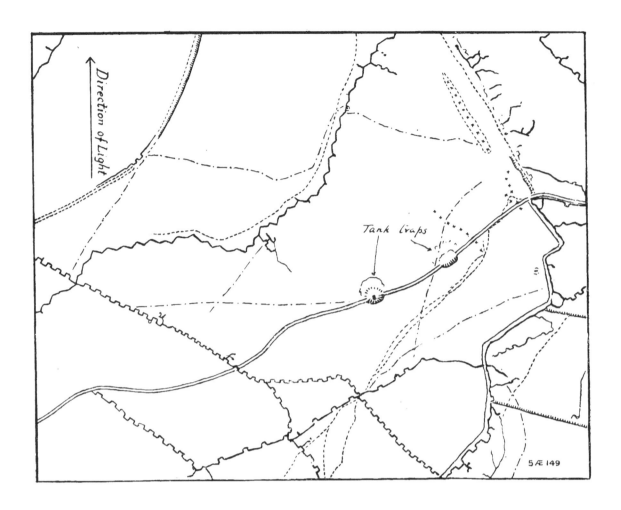

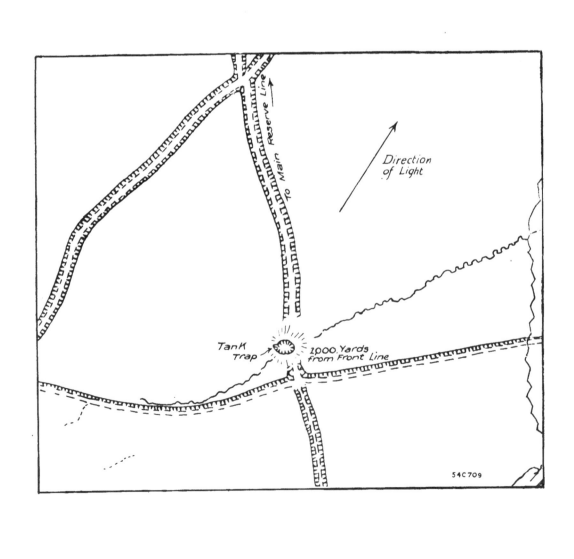

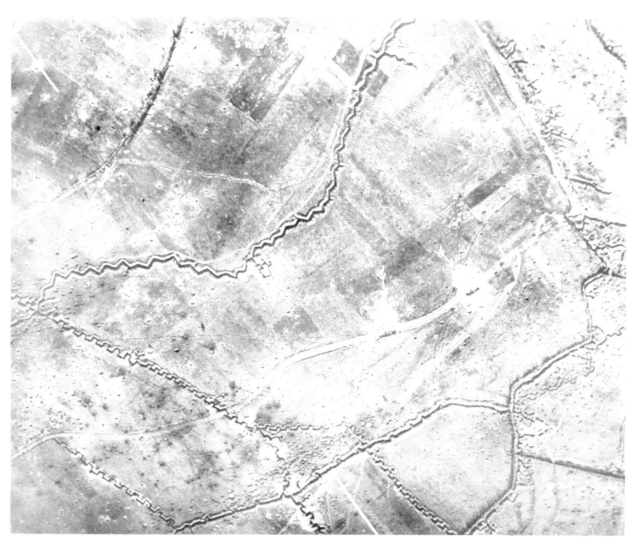

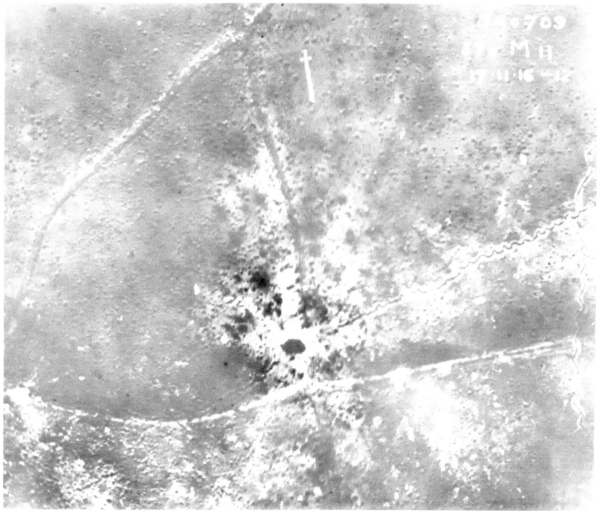

Plate 40.

TYPICAL CLOSE COUNTRY.

AREA :—Boesinghe to Ypres-Comines Canal.

Billets

Houses on main
street, with huts
in garden.

R.E Park
or stores

Hutments

Sheds

20 K 340

A A. gun empl?
for defence of →
MENIN

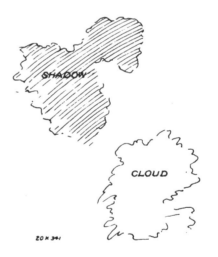

SHADOW

CLOUD

20 K 341

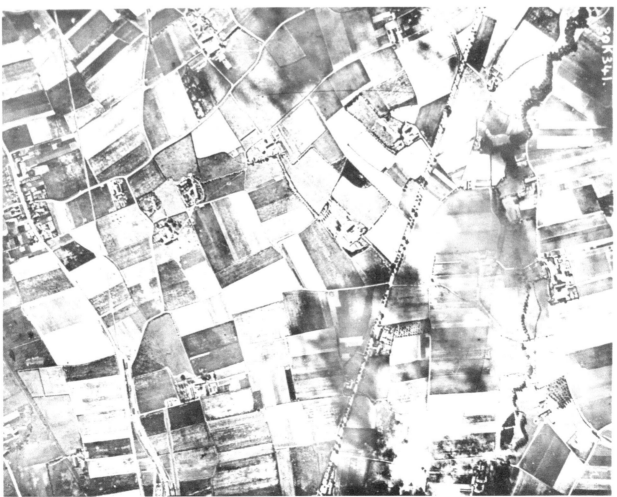

PLATE 41.

TRACKS.

IMPORTANT SUPPLY CENTRE.

AREA:—Boesinghe to Ypres-Comines Canal.

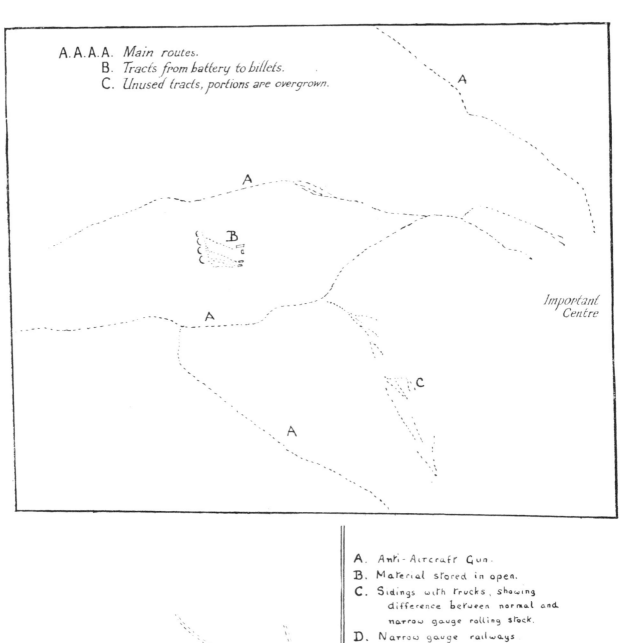

A.A.A.A. *Main routes.*
B. *Tracts from battery to billets.*
C. *Unused tracts, portions are overgrown.*

A

A

A

B

A

*Important
Centre*

C

A

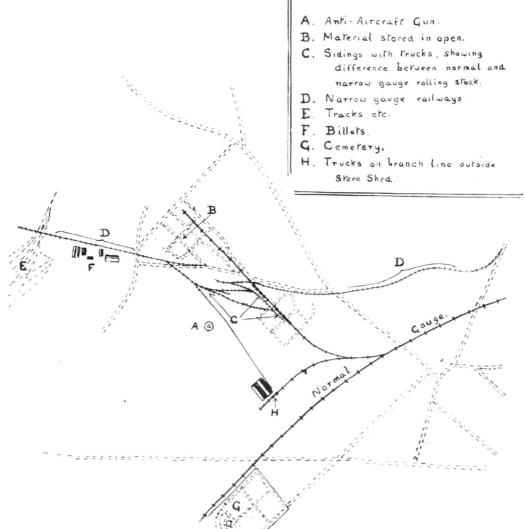

A. Anti-Aircraft Gun.
B. Material stored in open.
C. Sidings with trucks, showing
      difference between normal and
      narrow gauge rolling stock.
D. Narrow gauge railways
E. Tracks etc.
F. Billets.
G. Cemetery.
H. Trucks on branch line outside
      Store Shed.

B

D

E

F

D

A ⊙

C

H

Normal

Gauge.

G

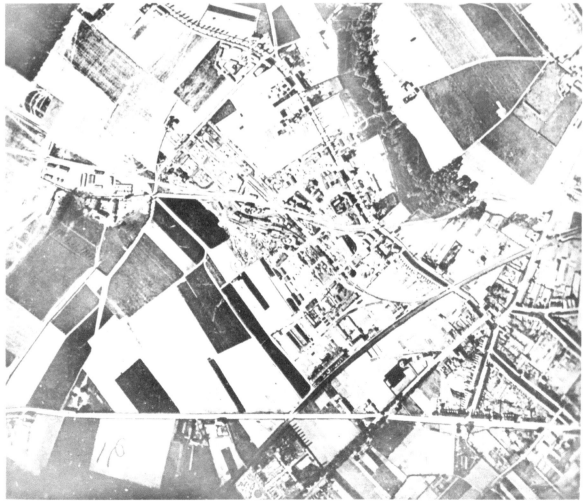

PLATE 42.

SUPPLY CENTRE.

HOSTILE AERODROME.

AREA :—Boesinghe to Ypres-Comines Canal.

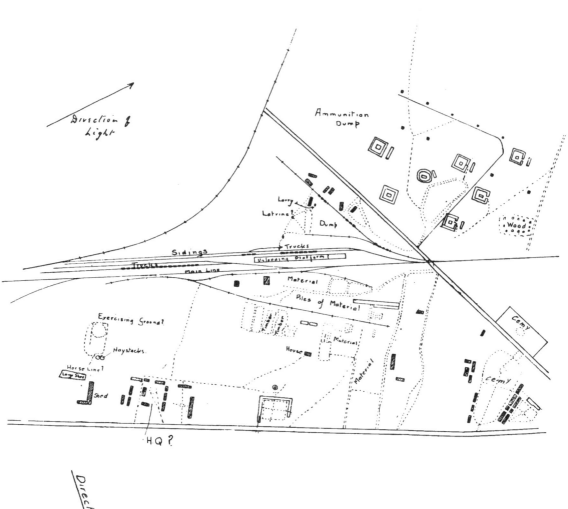

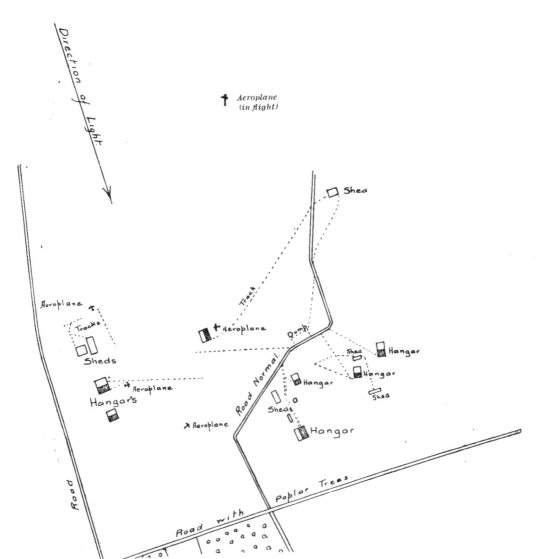

PLATE 43.

BOMBING RAIDS.

AREA :—River Scarpe to River Ancre.

Bombing Raids

A. Train hit and burning
△ Dump

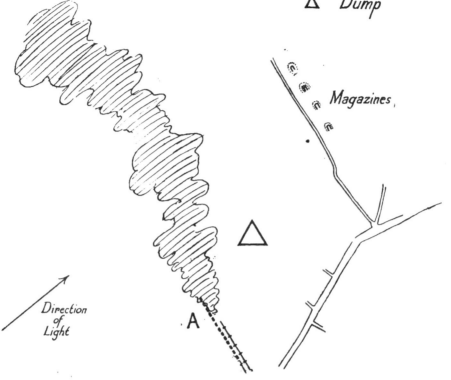

Magazines

△

Direction
of
Light

A

Heavy
bomb

↳ Landing T

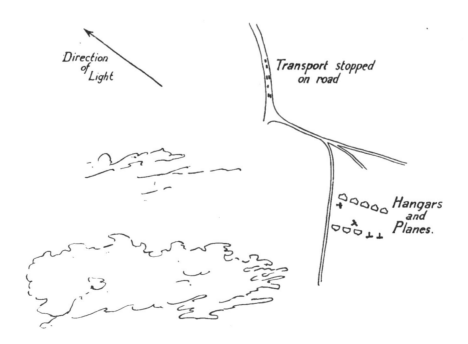

Direction
of
Light

Transport stopped
on road

Hangars
and
Planes.

PLATE 44.

OBLIQUE AND VERTICAL PHOTOGRAPHS
OF THE SAME AREA.

AREA :—River Ancre to River Somme.

1. Butte de
   Warlencourt.
2. Quarry.
3. Dump.
4. Normal gauge
   line from dump
   to **Bapaume**.
5. Trench.

Example of
Oblique and
Vertical
Photographs
covering
the same
area.

PLATE 45.

STEREOSCOPIC VIEWER.

STEREOSCOPIC VIEWER
For use with direct contact
prints mounted on a card.

Simple eye pieces for use
with ordinary unmounted
prints.

PLATE 46.

STEREOSCOPIC SLIDES.

*Direct contact prints mounted
for the stereoscopic viewer.*

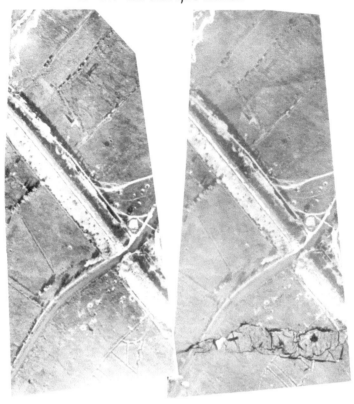

*Ordinary enlargements mounted
for the simple eye pieces.*

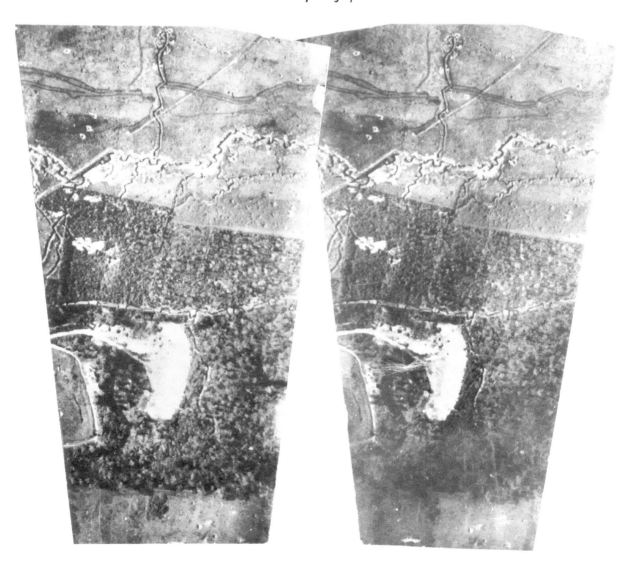

ND - #0231 - 270225 - C0 - 297/210/9 - PB - 9781908487858 - Matt Lamination